MASTER SORAI'S RESPONSALS

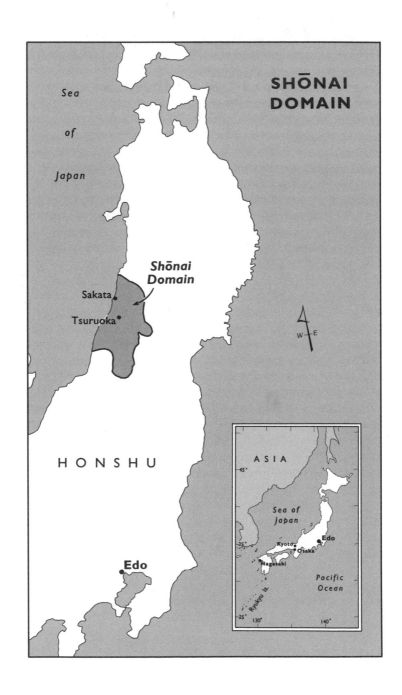

SHŌNAI
DOMAIN

Sea

of

Japan

*Shōnai
Domain*

Sakata

Tsuruoka

N
W — E

HONSHU

Edo

ASIA

45°

Sea
of
Japan

35°

Kyoto
Osaka

Edo

Nagasaki

Pacific
Ocean

Ryukyu Is.

25°   130°

140°

MASTER SORAI'S RESPONSALS

AN ANNOTATED TRANSLATION OF

Sorai sensei tōmonsho

Samuel Hideo Yamashita

UNIVERSITY OF HAWAII PRESS

HONOLULU

B 5244
.0353
T6613
1994

© 1994 University of Hawaii Press
All rights reserved
Printed in the United States of America

94 95 96 97 98 99   5 4 3 2 1

Library of Congress Cataloging-in-Publication Data
Ogyū, Sorai, 1666–1728.
[Tōmonsho. English]
Master Sorai's responsals : an annotated translation of Sorai
Sensei Tōmonsho / translator Samuel Hideo Yamashita.
p.   cm.
Includes index.
ISBN 0–8248–1570–X
I. Yamashita, Samuel Hideo, 1946– . II. Title.
B5244.0353T6613   1994
181'.12—dc20   94-15416
CIP

Publication of this book has been assisted
by a grant from the Japan Foundation.

University of Hawaii Press books are printed on
acid-free paper and meet the guidelines for
permanence and durability of the Council
on Library Resources

Designed by Kenneth Miyamoto

To My Parents

CONTENTS

ACKNOWLEDGMENTS

Master Sorai's Responsals would never have found its way into print without the help of many scholars and friends, both in Japan and the United States. My deepest debts are to my teachers—Roger Hackett, William Hauser, and Minamoto Ryōen—who were unstinting in their support and encouragement. William Hauser and Herman Ooms read the entire manuscript at a critical point and offered extremely helpful advice about how I might revise it. I also owe much to Bitō Masahide, Kojima Yasunori, and Koike Yoshiaki, who met with me from time to time and always had answers to my questions, even the strange and impertinent ones. Bruce Coats, Jan Goodwin, Stanleigh Jones, Dorinne Kondo, Lynne Miyake, Peter Nosco, and Eri Yasuhara read an early version of my introduction and made valuable suggestions for revision. No one, however, worked harder and gave more generously of his time than Hiraishi Naoaki, who went over the penultimate draft of my translation page by page, line by line, and word by word. Without his vast and deep knowledge of Sorai's life and writings, *Master Sorai's Responsals* would be a less faithful translation.

It was my good fortune to have had the help of two very fine editors. My wife, Margaret Barrows Yamashita, read various versions of the manuscript with her professional editor's eye and untangled the knots in my prose, insisted on consistency, and added polish to the translation. And Patricia Crosby not only oversaw the publication of *Master Sorai's Responsals* but did everything possible to make it the book I hoped it would be.

I would like to thank Sakai Tadahisa of the Shidōkan Museum in Tsuruoka, Japan, for allowing me to use the portrait of Ogyū Sorai that appears on the jacket of this book. It is housed in the museum's permanent collection. I am grateful to Yamagata Shinkō of Chūō Kōronsha and Kojima Yasunori for their help with this matter.

Finally, the research committee and the Office of the Dean at Pomona College funded this project at several stages, enabling me to make several trips to Tokyo, to have a map of Shōnai domain made, and to hire Sanjay Anand, Carolyn Iyoya, Katie Copeland, Brian Hudgens, and Chris Garcia to do the word processing for the early drafts.

Ogyū Sorai:
His Life, Context,
and Interpreters

Sometime around 1720, a Confucian scholar named Ogyū Sorai began to correspond with two young warriors in a small feudal domain in northwestern Japan. The two men, Mizuno Genrō and Hikita Yakara, sent him letters filled with queries about a range of topics—courage, military tactics, the meaning of key Confucian terms, finding talented individuals for the domain's bureaucracy, economic profit, Buddhism, spirits, and, above all, how to study the Confucian classics—and Sorai obligingly responded, writing what were more like scholarly disquisitions than letters. The correspondence lasted for nearly five years, and Sorai's letters—thirty-five in all—were published in 1727 as *Sorai sensei tōmonsho,* which I am translating here as "Master Sorai's Responsals."[1]

The importance of these letters is obvious. Sorai was a leading Confucian scholar of the day, some would say *the* leading scholar. He was the architect of a series of philosophical innovations of enormous significance, and these letters give us insights into these changes and much else that happened, intellectually, in the latter half of the eighteenth century. The letters also tell us much about Sorai as a thinker. Written just as he completed his most famous philosophical works—*Distinguishing the Way (Bendō)* and *Distinguishing Names (Benmei)*

1. Hiraishi Naoaki, a leading expert on Sorai, believes that only the last three of the thirty-five letters comprising *Master Sorai's Responsals* were written to Mizuno and Hikita. The others, he argues, were merely written in an epistolary style. Hiraishi suggested to me that Sorai saw this work as an introduction to his philosophy and comparable to Itō Jinsai's *A Boy's Questions (Dōjimon),* published in 1720. See Hiraishi Naoaki, "Kenkyū nōto—'Sorai sensei tōmonsho' kō: Keiten chūshaku to seisaku teigen no aida," *Shakai kagaku kenkyū* 45(1993): 217–237.

—and was working on his memorials on statecraft—*A Proposal for a Great Peace (Taiheisaku)* and *A Discourse on Government (Seidan)*—his letters tell us what he was thinking at this moment: what he thought about his own age, what worried him, what irked him, and what gave him cause for hope.[2]

These letters also reveal Sorai as a person. They confirm his vast erudition: he was well versed in Chinese history, philosophy, religion, military science, medicine, and belles lettres and could hold forth on everything from archaic Chinese divination to Sung poetry and prose and even write pieces in classical Chinese that mimicked particular styles or echoed specific poems. They demonstrate, too, that Sorai, although something of a Sinophile, was equally comfortable discussing minor warrior generals from his country's own Warring States period or contemporary systems of taxation. But the letters also show us a glimpse of his temperament: he was by turns earnest, frank, occasionally impatient, sometimes condescending, and, above all, self-assured. Much of his advice to Mizuno and Hikita, for example, is buttressed by nothing more than his own personal vision. No wonder, then, that he had such disdain for those who disagreed with him and those who were less learned and "could never be made to understand."

Sorai's letters are of interest for other reasons as well. We learn a lot about the affairs of small domains—in this case, the Shōnai domain—and their problems. The letters confirm that Shōnai, five years into the Kyōhō period (1716–1736), was experiencing many of the same fiscal and administrative problems as other domains and that domain officials were searching for solutions. Moreover, the correspondence leads us into the fierce debate between scholars loyal to Neo-Confucian teachings and their opponents, a debate that began in the 1660s and was still raging in the 1720s. As is well known, Sorai had profound misgivings about the several varieties of Neo-Confucianism popular in his day, and in these letters he gives his reasons. And,

2. Olof Lidin has translated *Distinguishing the Way* into English. See *Ogyū Sorai's Distinguishing the Way: An Annotated Translation of the Bendō* (Tokyo: Sophia University Press, 1970). Parts of *A Discourse on Government* are available in English translation in J. R. McEwan, *The Political Writings of Ogyū Sorai*, University of Cambridge Oriental Publications, no. 7 (Cambridge: Cambridge University Press, 1962). See also Richard Minear, "Ogyū Sorai's *Instructions for Students:* A Translation and Commentary," *Harvard Journal of Asiatic Studies* 36(1976):5–81, for a translation of Sorai's *Gakusoku*.

finally, the letters are a good introduction to his ideas. Apparently his contemporaries saw them in this light and read them as "a primer and outline of Sorai's teachings that conveyed his theories and ideas with utmost lucidity," and it may be, as some have suggested, that the letters should be read as a commentary on Sorai's two most famous works—*Distinguishing the Way* and *Distinguishing Names*—or, at the very least, as a popularized version.[3]

Ogyū Sorai: A Biography

Sorai was a native of Edo, born there in 1666, the second son of Ogyū Hoan, personal physician to Tokugawa Tsunayoshi, lord of the Tatebayashi domain and later shogun. He grew up in comfortable surroundings near the shogun's castle and sometimes accompanied his father on his rounds and on one occasion even met the shogun's wife. Sorai was first educated at home by his father, who taught him to read and write classical Chinese, and then he studied briefly at the Confucian academy run by the Hayashi family. His education at the Hayashi school was interrupted when the Ogyū family was summarily banished from Edo in 1679 for reasons that still are not clear. They were taken in by relatives who lived about seventy miles away in Honnō, a remote coastal village in Kazusa province. Conditions in Honnō, a community of farmers, fishermen, and woodcutters, were primitive, and the family found themselves without the amenities of urban life, without elegant and learned company, and, above all, without books. Sorai's mother died in 1680. In 1692, the shogun pardoned Hoan, and the family, after a decade or so away from Edo, was allowed to return. Hoan once again served as the shogun's physician.[4]

---

3. Imanaka Kanshi, *Soraigaku no kisoteki kenkyū* (Tokyo: Yoshikawa Kōbunkan, 1966), p. 253; Nakamura Yukihiko, "Kaidai," *Nihon koten bungaku taikei* (Tokyo: Iwanami Shoten, 1966), 94:26 (hereafter cited as *NKBT*); and Shimada Kenji, "Kaidai-hanrei," *Ogyū Sorai zenshū,* edited by Maruyama Masao and Yoshikawa Kōjirō (Tokyo: Mizusu Shobō, 1974), 1:620 (hereafter cited as *MOSZ*).

4. Hiraishi Naoaki, *Ogyū Sorai nempukō* (Tokyo: Heibonsha, 1984), pp. 172–174. This is the best and most authoritative source of biographical information on Sorai. See also Olof Lidin, *The Life of Ogyū Sorai: A Tokugawa Confucian Philosopher,* Scandinavian Institute of Asian Studies Monograph Series, no. 19 (Lund, Sweden: Student Litteratur, 1973).

Exactly when Sorai returned to Edo is unclear. He may have returned with his father in 1692 or, as Hiraishi Naoaki and others suggest, two years earlier, in 1690. Certainly the latter date is a possibility, since the authorities often allowed families of those banished from Edo to return early. This may have been the case with Sorai.[5] Once back in Edo, he moved to the Shiba area in the southern suburbs of Edo and tried to make a living as a teacher. He gave lectures on the Chinese classics and, although virtually unknown, slowly attracted a following. In 1696, when he was still struggling to establish himself, he came to the attention of Yanagisawa Yasuaki (known as Yoshiyasu after 1704), chamberlain and confidant of the fifth shogun, Tokugawa Tsunayoshi. When Yanagisawa house Confucians interviewed the young teacher, Sorai impressed them with his knowledge and was hired on the spot. Joining the platoon of poets, artists, and scholars serving Yoshiyasu, he performed a variety of tasks for his new employer ranging from punctuating Chinese texts to giving public lectures on Confucian topics. He often was present when the shogun visited Yoshiyasu and frequently was asked to lecture or to join the poetry meets held on these occasions. Sorai was also a regular auditor at the shogun's lectures on the Chinese classics. After he had served Yoshiyasu for fourteen years, he retired from active service in 1709.

After his retirement, Sorai opened a school, the Miscanthus Patch Academy (Ken'en-juku), in Kayabachō, not far from Nihonbashi, and over the next decade established himself as a leading Confucian teacher. Thus by the time he began corresponding with Mizuno and Hikita, he was well known as a teacher and had a number of students, many of whom had come great distances to study with him. Some were sent by their parents; others came at the urging of their teachers, who were Sorai's associates or disciples; a few were drawn by accounts of his school and his unusual pedagogy. Instruction at the Miscanthus Patch Academy centered not on ethical matters, as it did in most other Confucian academies, but on belles lettres, particularly Chinese classical prose and medieval poetry. Moreover, Sorai chose not to lecture to his students but, rather, to have them write poetry and prose compositions in imitation of Chinese models. For this he

5. Hiraishi, personal communication.

was roundly criticized by other teachers, who regarded this method as blatant indifference to the ethical and political matters that had long been a staple of Confucian education. But these attacks were also prompted by Sorai's success, for by this time his students had begun to attract considerable attention for their literary skills.

Sorai's fame had other sources. A collection of his essays, *Jottings from a Miscanthus Patch (Ken'en zuihitsu)*, published in 1714, established him as a fierce critic of Neo-Confucianism and earned him a national reputation. Indeed, many who came to study with him either had read these essays or had heard others talk about Sorai as a rising scholar. Not long afterward he began to formulate his highly original—some would say eccentric—vision of Confucianism, calling for the recovery of the "lost meanings" of the Chinese classics and the revival of an archaic Chinese civilization. This vision appears in nearly everything Sorai wrote in the late 1710s, particularly *Distinguishing the Way* and *Distinguishing Names*, and suffuses the letters in *Master Sorai's Responsals*.

Sorai's success brought him to the attention of the eighth shogun, Tokugawa Yoshimune, who, in 1720, began sending trusted senior retainers to solicit his opinions on contemporary issues. In these meetings, held secretly, Sorai was presented with questions and vexing problems and was expected, in his capacity as a "secret consultant," to offer answers and advance recommendations as best he could. The queries touched on all the pressing problems of the day: the hiring of talented people, the commercialization of the national economy, the decadence of urban life, the decline of the warrior class, currency reform, and a host of other issues. In addition to these exchanges, Sorai was commissioned to write two memorials in which he made recommendations for policy. The first, *A Proposal for a Great Peace*, was a general and somewhat philosophical response to a series of consultations that began in either 1716 or 1721. The second, *A Discourse on Government*, a long and detailed four-volume, issue-by-issue response, was written in 1725. Both memorials reveal as much about contemporary problems as they do about Sorai's thinking on these problems. The surest proof that his opinions were valued is that some of his recommendations were eventually implemented and, indeed, he was about to enter the shogun's service when he died in 1728.

Sorai and the Shōnai Domain

We know relatively little about Mizuno and Hikita and are not even
certain about their involvement in the correspondence with Sorai, as
they are never referred to by name in the letters. It was Yuasa Jōzan
(1708–1781) who first reported that "the people asking the questions
in *Responsals* were two of Sakai Saemon Joden's officials, Mizuno
Yohyōei [Genrō] and Hikita Yakara by name."[6] We do know that
Mizuno and Hikita were warriors from Shōnai domain, a small *fudai*
fief located on the Japan Sea coast in Dewa province. Mizuno, the
older of the pair, was born in 1692 into a high-ranking warrior family. His father rose to be a house elder, and Mizuno inherited his
father's position, becoming a house elder in 1740 or 1742. Hikita,
who was born in 1700 and thus was eight years younger than
Mizuno, was the second son of a high-ranking warrior named Matsu-
daira Tōhachirō. In 1720, he was adopted by Hikita Tatewaki and
thus took the Hikita name. He attained the position of captain of the
guard but died suddenly in 1738.[7]

Mizuno and Hikita began studying Neo-Confucian philosophy
with Katō Daini, the founder of Confucian studies in Shōnai. Because
Katō had been a student of Satō Naokata, Mizuno and Hikita probably read Satō's writings, those of Satō's teacher, Yamazaki Ansai
(1618–1682), and even some of Chu Hsi (1130–1200), who was
deeply revered in Ansai's Kimon school. Hikita is thought to have
studied with Naokata during a brief period of residence in Edo, probably between 1715 and 1716.[8] At some point in the late 1710s or
early 1720s, Mizuno and Hikita turned from Chu Hsi and the Kimon
school's teachings to those of Sorai.

Exactly what made Mizuno and Hikita decide to write to Sorai is
not clear. Sorai was well enough known by the late 1710s that they
might have written to him on their own initiative. Or perhaps they
had heard of him from their teachers or friends in Shōnai and wrote
on their recommendation, although the popularity there of the Kimon

6. *Ken'en zatsuwa,* quoted in Imanaka, *Soraigaku no kisoteki kenkyū,* p. 335.
7. Yamagata Ken, comp., *Yamagata ken-shi* (Yamagata: Ōba Insatsu Kabushiki
Kaisha, 1985), 2:963–964; Saitō Shōichi, *Shōnai-han* (Tokyo: Yoshikawa Kōbunkan, 1990), *Nihon rekishi sōsho,* no. 43, pp. 192–193.
8. Imanaka, *Soraigaku no kisoteki kenkyū,* p. 340; Saitō, *Shōnai-han,* p. 192;
and *Hanshi daijiten* (Tokyo: Yusankaku, 1982 [1976]), 1:427.

school's teachings makes this unlikely. Because *Jottings from a Miscanthus Patch* was circulating throughout the country, Mizuno and Hikita may have discovered it on their own and been sufficiently intrigued by Sorai's reading of Neo-Confucianism and his criticisms of Itō Jinsai to write to him. But even this scenario would explain only half of the story and leave unanswered the other and more difficult half: why Sorai responded in the way that he did.

It seems unlikely that their relationship began casually. After all, Mizuno and Hikita were relatively young—Mizuno was in his late twenties, Hikita was in his late teens. Moreover, both were students of Kimon teachings, which Sorai by this time fiercely opposed, and so he would have been unlikely to carry on such an extensive correspondence with his opponents. Sorai did occasionally correspond with Neo-Confucian scholars—for example, Hori Keizan (1688–1757) and Asaka Tanpaku (1656–1737)—but both were well-established scholars when he began writing to them: Keizan was in his early thirties and serving the lord of Hiroshima domain; Tanpaku was an eminent scholar and head of the massive historiographical project undertaken by the Mito domain.[9] Most telling of all, however, Sorai was not in good health and hence jealously guarded his time. "I am now past fifty," he wrote in the late 1710s. "If I were not to work [at my task of popularizing the Way of the Sages and Early Kings] and to die without carrying it out, what of my Heaven-appointed destiny? This is why I devote all of my leisure hours to writing and thus repaying Heaven's grace."[10] In 1720 he reported in a letter to a friend that he had been sick for some time and that his condition was steadily worsening. "Fearing that I will die shortly [and vanish] like the first dew of the day," he wrote, "I work on *Distinguishing the Way* whenever my condition permits."[11] Sorai's acute sense of his own mortality suggests that he felt compelled to respond to the inquiries sent by Mizuno and Hikita. But compelled by whom?

My suspicion is that Mizuno and Hikita first contacted, and then corresponded with, Sorai on behalf of senior officials in Shōnai or even their lord, Sakai Tadazane. The author of *Kansan yoroku,* pub-

9. See Ogyū Sorai, "Kutsu Keizan ni kotau," *Nihon shisō taikei* (Tokyo: Iwanami Shoten, 1973), 36:527–535 (hereafter cited as *NST*).

10. Sorai, *Bendō, NST,* 36:200.

11. Sorai, "Kōkoku ni atau [10]," quoted in Hiraishi, *Ogyū Sorai nempukō,* p. 124.

lished in 1782, contends that Mizuno and Hikata were not the only
ones sending questions to Sorai. Three things suggest that they were
writing on behalf of others. The first is the length and quality of
Sorai's letters and the duration of the correspondence—that is, Sorai
would not have corresponded with the two young warriors in the way
that he did and for as long as he did without the pressure of some
greater authority. Second, there is good reason to believe that Sakai
Tadazane knew Sorai. Because Tadazane spent ten years in Edo—
from 1694 to 1704—and apparently was a member of the group of
high-ranking warriors, scholars, artists, and poets who gathered
round the shogun Tsunayoshi, giving lectures on scholarly subjects,
holding debates in colloquial Chinese, and participating in the poetry
meets held frequently at Edo Castle or the residences of the shogun's
most trusted retainers. This was the group that Sorai joined after
entering Yanagisawa's service and through which he attracted the
attention and favor of his lord and the shogun. Like Sorai, Tadazane
lectured in the shogun's presence in 1695. Because he continued to
reside in Edo for twelve- to fourteen-month periods every eight
months, in accordance with the alternate attendance system, there
were ample opportunities for contact with Sorai.[12]

The third reason is that Tadazane was interested in Confucianism.
Although the Kimon school's teachings in Shōnai had a powerful
champion in Katō Daini—a house elder by the time the correspondence begins—Tadazane was open to other schools. In 12/1723, for
instance, he invited Muro Kyūsō (1658–1734), a leading Confucian
scholar from Matsunaga Sekigo's Bokumon school and a favorite of
the shogun Yoshimune, to lecture on the *Analects* at one of the Shōnai
residences in Edo. The lecture was expressly arranged for the benefit
of Tadazane's heir, Sakai Tadayori, who apparently was not very
enthusiastic and "retained nothing at all from the lecture."[13] Kyūsō
then was invited to give another lecture in 1725. Kyūsō also corresponded with a Shōnai retainer named Sugiyama, who may have been
writing on orders from his superiors, and sent him a copy of his commentary on the *Great Learning*.[14] The point, however, is that Tadazane's interest in Sorai is not surprising.

If Mizuno and Hikita wrote to Sorai on behalf of Shōnai, what

12. *Yamagata ken-shi*, 2:963; *Hanshi daijiten*, 1:427.
13. *Yamagata ken-shi*, 2:963.
14. Saitō, *Shōnai-han*, p. 191.

prompted them to do this? Why were Shōnai officials soliciting the recommendations of Confucian scholars? The answer is that Shōnai was in the midst of a crisis. In 8/1720, swarms of flying insects descended on fields in Shōnai and elsewhere, threatening the crops that were soon to be harvested and thus the livelihood of all in the domain. Despite the best efforts of the local population to drive away the pests, called "swarming bugs" (J. *unka mushi*), they destroyed the fall harvest, and this had several predictable effects.[15] The first was food shortages in the domain's two major cities and the surrounding countryside as well. The authorities responded by setting up soup kitchens in Tsuruoka (the domain's capital) and Sakata (the main port town) and relief centers in rural areas to reach those without food, and they offered emergency loans to the most marginal elements of the domain society, the pariah classes and the handicapped.[16] The disaster also led to reduced tax revenue, whose ramifications domain officials were quick to recognize.

Shōnai had just emerged from two extended periods of financial crisis. The first resulted from a massive reclamation project begun in the 1630s and 1640s to increase the domain's revenues. The project succeeded in adding sixteen thousand *koku* to the tax rolls, but it led to unexpected water and labor shortages.[17] It also left a larger surplus in the hands of rural cultivators, which they proceeded to sell, and the authorities responded by prohibiting merchants from entering villages to buy the excess produce.[18] Thus from the 1660s Shōnai had begun to experience fiscal problems. The second crisis was triggered by a poor harvest, which was the result of a series of natural calamities: a cold spell, a typhoon, and the eruption of Mount Fuji. An added burden was a Tokugawa order directing Shōnai to repair a section of the Tōkaidō—the highway that ran from Edo to Kyoto and Osaka—which had been damaged during the typhoon. The domain's authorities used all possible methods and institutions: they issued the usual exhortations to the population, urging them to be frugal; they increased taxes; and they levied what was known euphemistically as

15. *Yamagata ken-shi*, 2:740.
16. Ibid., 2:741.
17. A *koku* was a unit of measure used chiefly for rice and other grains. During the Tokugawa period, one *koku* was equivalent to 5.12 U.S. bushels. Warriors' salaries and landholdings were measured in *koku*.
18. Hanshi Kenkyūkai, comp., *Hanshi jiten* (Tokyo: Akita Shoten, 1976), p. 61.

"offered rice" (J. *agemai*), a levy that automatically reduced warriors' salaries at the rate of one hundred *hyō* for every hundred *koku* of rice. The domain had resorted to the "offered rice" tax twice before— in 1690 and in 1706—and it had not been very popular. Although Shōnai retainers vigorously protested its reinstitution in 1707, it did provide the revenue that the domain needed to cope with the shortfall and meet the costs of the Tōkaidō project.[19] And so, in the early 1700s, Shōnai—like so many other domains and even the Tokugawa themselves—was in financial distress. And it was not long after the crisis of the summer of 1720 that Mizuno and Hikita may have first written to Sorai.[20]

The content of the letters confirms this dating. Most deal with what Sorai called "political affairs." The first nine letters, however, treat an assortment of topics: they begin with Sorai's definition of the "way" (letters 1 to 4), continue with his views of learning (5 and 6) and courage (7), and conclude with a discussion of Neo-Confucian metaphysics (8) and Buddhism (9).[21] The range of topics in these initial letters suggests that Sorai's questioners were feeling him out, perhaps even testing him. In the tenth letter the discussion suddenly turns to "political affairs," and virtually nothing else is discussed in the next fifteen letters, thereby revealing the real rationale for the correspondence. Not surprisingly, these letters address issues salient to a domain in distress: the search for talented officeholders (letters 11 to 14), local administration (15 and 16), profit as a policy issue (17), retainers' loyalty (18), reform (19), the population at large and their relationship with the ruler (22 and 24), and remonstration with rulers (25).

The discussion then shifts in the twenty-sixth letter to ethical issues, beginning with Sorai's questioners worrying about their "unusually unpleasant dispositions." Sorai responds by commending them for

19. *Yamagata ken-shi*, 2:738–739; Saitō, *Shōnai-han*, pp. 84–86.

20. Most modern scholars believe that Sorai began the correspondence around 1720 or 1721. See Imanaka, *Soraigaku no kisoteki kenkyū*, and Maruyama Masao, "Taiheisakukō," *NST*, 36:627.

In a personal communication, Hiraishi Naoaki agrees that Sorai probably began writing the letters in 1720–1721 but believes that the catalysts were the publication of Itō Jinsai's *A Boy's Questions* in 1720 and Sorai's work on *A Proposal for a Great Peace*, which was completed by 1721.

21. Modern editions of *Master Sorai's Responsals* do not number the letters. They simply divide the text into three sections—*jō-chū-ge*—and expect readers to know when one letter ends and another begins from the term *ijō*, which is conventionally used at the end of a letter. Here I number the letters.

"acknowledging their faults" but warns that "this is not a very healthy way to see yourselves." Why? Because human nature cannot be changed; it can only be refined. The letters continue with a discussion of self-cultivation (letter 27), the performance of virtue (28), and the study of Chinese prose and poetry as a form of refinement (29). The next five letters treat a potpourri of topics: divination (30), the way of the warrior (31), the Way of the Sages and Early Kings (33 and 35), and a series of educational questions, including what to teach officeholders of middling intelligence (32), how one should learn classical Chinese (33), and why mastering archaic, Chinese literary styles is important (34).

In the spring of 1724, Hattori Nankaku (1683–1759), one of Sorai's leading disciples, wrote a preface for the letters, which suggests that they were being readied for publication. Nankaku had served as the copyist all through the correspondence and apparently kept copies of Sorai's letters, which he and another disciple, Nemoto Sonshi (1699–1764), secretly edited. It was probably they, and not Sorai, who first thought of publishing the correspondence. After all, Sorai's only publications were *A Guide to Translation (Yakubun sentei)* and *Jottings from a Miscanthus Patch,* which represented earlier interests and views long since abandoned. Before this could be done, however, Sorai wrote three more letters in the late summer and early fall of 1725.[22]

Sorai met one of his questioners—Hikita—for the first time in the spring or summer of 1726.[23] It appears that Hikita and Mizuno asked at some point to be allowed to "enter" Sorai's school. Hikita's visit may have been prompted by Sorai's complaint at the beginning of the first of these three additional letters about the difficulties of discussing weighty matters such as "styles of learning" by letter. The missive begins: "You inquired about styles of learning, but this is a hard issue to discuss thoroughly by letter. This is why I have always refused to accept entrance gifts sent from afar. For some years now I have been the recipient of your considerable attention and have done as you wished. Your latest letter, however, perplexes me."[24] It continues:

22. Shimada, "Kaidai-hanrei," *MOSZ,* 1:620; Nakamura, "Kaidai," *NKBT,* 94:26; and Hiraishi, *Ogyū Sorai nempukō,* p. 146.
23. Hiraishi, personal communication.
24. Sorai, *Sorai sensei tōmonsho,* in *Nihon rinri ihen,* edited by Inoue Tetsujirō and Kanie Yoshimaru (Kyoto: Rinsen, 1970), 6:186–189 (hereafter cited as *NRI*).

In the first place, communicating over great distances is obviously difficult. This is why all of Confucius' disciples went to study with him at some point. When one enters a school, one encounters what might be called the "school style," and after being steeped in that school style through various means, one understands quite a lot. The ancient saying "making teachers of one's friends" suggests that it is less a teacher's instructions than the encouragement of friends that broadens one's knowledge and advances one's studies. One cannot say, for example, that the lessons given at present to lords and others of high rank go very well: they employ good teachers and study with them, but because of their rank and wealth, they have no friends, and it seems clear that no matter what they study, they will never master it. Having academic friends and being steeped in a school style is the first issue. Thus, your being so far away obviously impedes our communication.

Given your abiding interest, however, I should like to suggest something that might serve as a substitute for teachers and friends. Although not a perfect substitute, if you use it, your interest will be rewarded. That substitute for teachers and friends is books. Avoiding friends who will not help and approaching those who will is the way to make friends. Thus your eyes should not fall on books that will not help; you should immerse yourself in books that will. There is no other substitute for teachers and friends.[25]

Sorai's nagging worked; Hikita went to Edo.

Ironically, Sorai had indicated in the last of the three letters he wrote in the fall of 1725 that the correspondence would soon end, as there were now more urgent demands on his time. "From now on," he explained, "I will be busier, and detailed responses will be impossible."[26] What he did not mention is that three months earlier, the Tokugawa authorities had ordered him to submit his recommendations on institutional reform. He had been working on this project all through the fall, even as he continued to correspond with Mizuno and Hikita, and completed it in 1726 or 1727.[27] The fruit of his labors was *A Discourse on Government,* a four-volume memorial that analyzed the contemporary situation and offered highly detailed recommendations. It was the opportunity that Sorai had waited for: a chance to translate his own personal vision into policy.

25. Ibid.
26. Ibid.
27. Hiraishi, *Ogyū Sorai nempukō,* pp. 150–152, 263.

That his correspondence with Mizuno and Hikita was about to end was obvious. Sorai's last letter is full of final words of advice, opening with a warning about the hazards of self-study and advice about how to manage on one's own:

> As for the methods of learning and the course to be followed, you will lose your way unless you have the guidance of those who are well versed in such matters. If what I am teaching you seems puzzling, it is best to keep asking about it. After making your inquiries, if you still do not understand, try practicing what you have learned. Or you might follow my teachings for a time even if you do not understand them and thus learn them in this way. In any event, if what I say proves to be wrong in the end, it is perfectly reasonable for you to reject it. Then, again, I am not insisting that you follow my teachings.[28]

And to ensure that Mizuno and Hikita got his point, Sorai repeats his advice at the end of the letter: "You might reread my responses for half a year or so, studying and practicing what I have suggested. When you have done that, the logic of my advice will be clear." He closes with a suggestion that "when you think that you might want to follow my methods and engage in scholarship, you should have a bookseller make copies of *Distinguishing the Way* and *Distinguishing Names* and send them to you. If you do not do this, I believe that you will encourage disagreement and fail to make progress."[29]

When Sorai wrote the last letter, he did not know whether he would ever meet the pair. His meeting with Hikita appears to have occurred at some point after 10/3/1725, the date of his last letter. Hiraishi believes that they met in the spring or summer of 1726.[30] Hikita was still in Edo in 1/1727, a full month and a half before Tadazane's next period of alternate attendance was to begin. We know this because in that month he sent to Shōnai a letter and representative works by Sorai and his disciples, including a draft of the letters that four months later would be published as *Master Sorai's Responsals*. This letter and shipment of books suggest that Hikita had been permitted to stay in Edo for most of 1726 and into 1727 and had enrolled at the Miscanthus Patch Academy. We know for certain that he studied there at some point, for Sorai once wrote: "Master Hitsu [Hikita] and

28. Sorai, *Sorai sensei tōmonsho*, NRI, 6:191.
29. Ibid., p. 203.
30. Hiraishi, personal communication.

16 Ogyū Sorai

his friend Master Sui [Mizuno] found pleasure in the Way of the
Sages, sent boiled meat a thousand miles, and *while [Hikita] served in
the capital, I saw him morning and evening continuously*" (my italics).[31] And by the time Hikita left Edo in 5/1727, he seems to have
become a full-fledged member of Sorai's school and well enough
accepted that Dazai Shundai (1680–1747), one of Sorai's leading disciples, wrote a preface in his honor.[32]

Sorai's Philosophy

Upon his return to Shōnai, Hikita found that he and Mizuno were in
a minority. "Everyone in the domain and all of the upper-ranking
warriors were Neo-Confucians," they reported to Sorai, "and it was
just the two of them alone" who favored Sorai's philosophy, although
"recently seven or eight individuals whose views are sympathetic with
ours have emerged."[33] Sorai seems to have anticipated that Hikita and
Mizuno would be in a minority, as his last three letters deal almost
exclusively with Neo-Confucianism and disclose his animus for Chu
Hsi and those who followed him. In his last letter, Sorai presents his
four main objections to Neo-Confucianism. First, it prevented one
from mastering the language of the Chinese classics, because "Chu
Hsi's [interpretation] of certain passages in the classics diverged from
those found elsewhere" and departed from the original meanings of
those texts.[34] Second, studying Neo-Confucianism ruined one's literary style. As Sorai argued ad nauseam in his later writings, Neo-
Confucians preferred what he called an "argumentative style" to a
"descriptive style." As the latter was "the real stuff of literary style,"
as he put it, Neo-Confucians were greatly handicapped as writers. He
warned Mizuno and Hikita: if you continue to study Neo-Confucianism, "your writing will change, and no matter how much you prac-

31. Imanaka, *Soraigaku no kisoteki kenkyū*, p. 335.
32. Hiraishi, *Ogyū Sorai nempukō*, p. 161.
33. "Tōmonsho fukan—ōfuku shokan," *MOSZ*, 1:495. In a personal communication, Hiraishi indicated that he believes there was less opposition to Sorai's
views than one may think given Katō Daini's ties with the Kimon school of
Yamazaki Ansai. Katō, in fact, may have agreed with Sorai's insistence that classical texts be read in unpunctuated form. Hiraishi's evidence is a letter written by
Mizuno and Hikita to their lord, Sakai Tadazane, in 1727 that contains Katō's
comments in the margins.
34. Sorai, *Sorai sensei tōmonsho*, NRI, 6:200.

tice, it will resemble commentaries, and you will find it impossible to write in a true literary style."[35] Sorai's third objection to Neo-Confucianism was that it fostered misreadings of the Chinese classics by introducing a new vocabulary—"words like 'principle,' 'material force,' 'heavenly principle,' and 'human desire'"—and "adding a layer of meaning to the Way of the Sages."[36]

Finally, Neo-Confucianism could not be commended owing to its unsalutary effect on one's character. "Those nurtured on their commentaries on the classics," Sorai pointed out, "sharply distinguish right and wrong, heterodox and orthodox; they want everything handled efficiently from beginning to end; and they often are arrogant. Many condemn elegance and literary finesse and have wretched personalities."[37] No doubt remembering that Mizuno and Hikita had studied Kimon school teachings, Sorai added: "You have probably heard the rumors about the character of Yamazaki Ansai and Asami Keisai. The problem is not just their unfortunate pedagogy; it has to do with the one-sidedness of their approach."[38] Elsewhere, Sorai criticizes the Neo-Confucians for seeking omniscience and not revering Heaven and its agents, the Sages and Early Kings. And he is fiercely critical of the forms of self-cultivation they prescribed—in his eyes, they were not only unclassical but also inadvisable, both physically and psychologically.

Although Sorai's animus for the Neo-Confucians is clear, exactly whom he had in mind is not. Until very recently, it was widely assumed that Neo-Confucian scholars of that period were utterly faithful to the views of Chu Hsi, the Sung dynasty (960–1279) philosopher regarded as the father of Neo-Confucianism. No doubt this is what Inoue Tetsujirō (1855–1944) meant when he described the first generation of Tokugawa Confucians as the "spiritual slaves" of Chu Hsi.[39] In any case, the majority of those studying the ancient learning scholars have subscribed to this notion of a pure Neo-Confucianism represented by Chu Hsi and believe that Sorai was consciously formulating his views against those of Chu Hsi. As evidence they cite the dramatic differ-

35. Ibid.
36. Ibid.
37. Ibid.
38. Ibid.
39. Inoue Tetsujirō, *Nihon kogakuha no tetsugaku* (Tokyo: Fuzambō, 1902), p. 598.

ences between the metaphysical views of Chu Hsi and the ancient learning scholars. And so whereas Chu Hsi advanced a dualistic ontology that distinguished transcendental and physical dimensions, Sorai, together with Yamaga Sokō (1622–1685) and Itō Jinsai (1627–1705), according to these scholars, created a monistic ontology that recognized only a physical dimension.[40] Thus, most modern scholars portray Sorai and the other ancient learning scholars as engaged in a dialogue with Chu Hsi and insist that their writings be seen in this light.

Not all modern scholars, however, have agreed. One of the first dissenters was Bitō Masahide. He discovered that the views of the conservative Neo-Confucian Yamazaki Ansai diverged from those of Chu Hsi, to whom Ansai was fiercely loyal, and this discovery led him to suggest that seventeenth-century Japanese Neo-Confucians may not have been as faithful to Chu Hsi as was commonly thought.[41] And Tahara Tsuguo, following Bitō's lead, declared that what was true of Yamazaki Ansai and his Kimon school was true also of Sorai, Sokō, and Jinsai, whose conception of Neo-Confucianism was hardly pure and indeed amounted to what Tahara called a "pseudo-Neo-Confucianism" (J. *giji shushigaku*).[42]

What, then, explains this apparent divergence of Chu Hsi's views and those of seventeenth-century Japanese Neo-Confucians? One view is that the pioneering Neo-Confucians did not accept Chu Hsi's philosophy on its own terms but, rather, in terms of "Japanese patterns of thought" (J. *nihonteki shii*).[43] This interpretation explains why these early Japanese Neo-Confucians did not fully understand Chu Hsi's views. It explains, for example, Hayashi Razan's peculiarly monistic interpretation of Chu Hsi's dualistic ontology. Similarly, the rather unorthodox conceptions of Neo-Confucianism held by Sokō, Sorai, and Jinsai suggest too that they did not oppose Chu Hsi's philosophy, as was argued earlier, but rather their own idiosyncratic con-

40. Maruyama Masao, *Nihon seiji shisōshi kenkyū* (Tokyo: Tokyo Daigaku Shuppankai, 1970), pp. 27, 49–50, 54–58, 82, 199–201; Matsumoto Sannosuke, "The Idea of Heaven: A Tokugawa Foundation for Natural Rights Theory," in *Japanese Thought in the Tokugawa Period: Methods and Metaphors,* edited by Tetsuo Najita and Irwin Scheiner (Chicago: University of Chicago Press, 1978), pp. 188–190.

41. Bitō Masahide, "Hōken rinri," in *Iwanami kōza nihon rekishi,* vol. 10: kinsei, no. 2 (Tokyo: Iwanami Shoten, 1963), pp. 304–306.

42. Tahara Tsuguo, *Tokugawa shisōshi kenkyū* (Tokyo: Miraisha, 1967), pp. 12, 19–21, 346.

43. Ibid., p. 492.

ception of Chu Hsi's views. This is a plausible explanation, accounting as it does for the obvious discrepancies between Chu Hsi's views and those attributed to him.[44]

A second answer is offered by the Japanese and American scholars inspired by the work of the late Abe Yoshio.[45] These scholars assert rather convincingly that the Neo-Confucianism popular in Japan in the seventeenth century was neither pure nor misunderstood. If it seems to diverge from the original formulation of Chu Hsi, this is because it was, in fact, different, and these differences reflect the evolution of Chu Hsi's views that took place in China and Korea after his death in 1200. And so instead of a single Neo-Confucianism, there were actually three variants of Neo-Confucianism represented in Japan, each of which was introduced to Japan from the continent during the sixteenth and seventeenth centuries. The first, which William Theodore deBary calls the "official state orthodoxy," was represented in the commentaries on the Confucian canon by Chu Hsi and his immediate predecessors. The second, the "philosophical orthodoxy," assumed two rather different forms: a highly introspective form that encouraged the pursuit, by means of meditation, of "the unitary principle in the dynamic integration of the conscious mind" and an alternative form that gave greater weight to the external and the physical and recommended extensive study as a means of apprehending principle. Both varieties had their advocates in China and Korea as well. The former was represented in China by Chu Hsi's teacher, Li T'ung (1088–1163), in Korea by Yi T'oegye (1501–1570), and in Japan by Fujiwara Seika (1561–1619); the latter was championed in China by a Ming Confucian named Lo Ch'in-shun (1465–1547) and in Japan by Hayashi Razan (1583–1657). The third variety of Neo-Confucianism was what deBary terms a "liberal orthodoxy" and identifies with independent Neo-Confucians like Wang Yang-ming (1472–1529). DeBary insists that both strains had an equal claim to orthodoxy and were "pure mainly in the sense of being faithful to the ambiguities of the Neo-Confucian tradition and carrying forward the development of the two main lines of thought that had already appeared in Ming China."[46]

44. Ibid. See also Imanaka, *Soraigaku no kisoteki kenkyū*, p. 128.

45. Abe Yoshio, *Nihon shushigaku to chōsen* (Tokyo: Tokyo Daigaku Shuppankai, 1965).

46. William Theodore deBary and Irene Bloom, eds., *Principle and Practicality: Essays in Neo-Confucianism and Practical Learning* (New York: Columbia University Press, 1979), pp. 16–21, 131–139. See also Abe, *Nihon shushigaku to chōsen*, pp. 493–496, 528–531.

DeBary situates Sorai within the context of these three varieties of Neo-Confucianism. He argues that Sorai rejected both the official state orthodoxy and the highly introspective variety of the philosophical orthodoxy and favored the type of philosophical orthodoxy that focused on the external world and called for study. DeBary is eager to show that Sorai, despite his opposition to Neo-Confucianism, remained a Neo-Confucian. Even his distrust of Neo-Confucian readings of the Confucian classics and his call for a return to the classics represent an option within what deBary calls the "Neo-Confucian synthesis."[47] Not only was it an option; it was articulated by Yen Yüan (1635–1704), who was "known for his outright rejection" of Neo-Confucianism. In any event, Sorai's antipathy for Neo-Confucianism is a recurring theme in everything he wrote after 1715, and thus its prominence in his letters to Mizuno and Hikita is not surprising. Even if one does not agree that Sorai was still a Neo-Confucian, it is clear that "Neo-Confucianism" is not a single phenomenon but a rubric encompassing several different philosophical strands and thinkers who embraced them.

Sorai's letters present three other themes that run through his later writings: his neoclassicism, his belief in a sentient Heaven, and his vitalistic cosmology. The first is his neoclassicism or, more accurately, Sinitic archaism. Sorai believed in the superiority of classical Chinese civilization, or what he called the "Way of the Sages and Early Kings." As he pointed out time and again, this superiority was based on the Sages' "extraordinarily deep, broad, and great knowledge," which enabled them "to create [culture and institutions] that accorded with the innate endowment of humans."[48] This meant that classical Chinese culture and institutions were not "natural," as some of Sorai's contemporaries argued, but "artificial," the product of human invention.[49] They were universal, as well, and thus "suitable for any age" and relevant even in his day as solutions to contemporary problems. "If one used the Way of the Sages," he promised, "even the provinces and the realm as they exist today would be ordered."

47. DeBary and Bloom, *Principle and Practicality*, p. 167.
48. Sorai, *Sorai sensei tōmonsho*, NRI, 6:197.
49. See Maruyama, *Nihon seiji shisōshi kenkyū*, pp. 193–318, and my "Nature and Artifice in the Writings of Ogyū Sorai (1666–1728)," in *Confucianism and Tokugawa Culture*, edited by Peter Nosco (Princeton: Princeton University Press, 1984), pp. 138–165.

Sorai truly believed this. When asked, first in 1721 and then in 1725, to advise the shogun Yoshimune on affairs of state, he agreed and presented his recommendations in *A Proposal for a Great Peace* and *A Discourse on Government*. Both address the pressing problems of the day: the shortage of talented officials;[50] shrinking government revenues;[51] and the commercialization of the national and regional economies and the resulting concentration of wealth in the hands of townsmen and the impoverishment of warriors.[52] What is striking about Sorai's recommendations is their self-conscious archaism. Consider his most famous proposal: the resettlement of the urban population in the countryside. It had as its locus classicus the account of the ancient Chinese well-field system found in the *Mencius* and which Sorai himself characterized as "a method that resettles the ten thousand people on the land [and] cultivates a warm relationship of mutual obligation among the people."[53] Sorai's recommendation for increasing the number of talented officials in the ranks of the Tokugawa administration is a second example. He called for the adoption of the "rank in merit" system (C. *hsün-chieh*, J. *kunkai*) that had been used in China in ancient times and allowed holders of a particular rank to hold not just one but several different posts. So, for example, a holder of the first and second ranks could hold senior councillorships and even the post of great councillor.[54] And to streamline the Tokugawa bureaucracy Sorai suggested adopting the Six Office (C. *liu-kuan*, J. *rokkan*) and Six Ministries (C. *liu-pu*, J. *roku-bu*) systems used in China from the Han dynasty (207 B.C.–A.D. 220).[55]

Moreover, because the Way of the Sages and Early Kings survived only in the Chinese classics, one had to learn the "ancient language" in which they were written. This meant learning to read the classics in

50. Hiraishi, *Ogyū Sorai nempukō*, p. 126.
51. Kitajima Masamoto, *Edo jidai* (Tokyo: Iwanami Shoten, 1964), pp. 123–124; Tsuji Tatsuya, "*Seidan* no shakaiteki haikei," *NST*, 36:773–774; and Ōishi Shinsaburō, *Genroku jidai* (Tokyo: Iwanami Shoten, 1973), p. 75.
52. Kitajima, *Edo jidai*, pp. 98–99; Tsuji, "*Seidan* no shakaiteki haikei," *NST*, 36:742–743.
53. Sorai, *Taiheisaku, NST*, 36:478–479. The well-field system is described in *Meng-tzu*, 3A:3. It was so named because it divided one square Chinese mile (C. *li*, J. *ri*) of land into nine squares 田, a formation that resembled the graph for well (C. *ching*, J. *ido*). In this arrangement, each of the outer squares was farmed by a family, and the central square was public land shared by all.
54. Sorai, *Seidan, NST*, 36:348.
55. Ibid., p. 353.

the original archaic Chinese without the help of latter-day commentaries, which Sorai characterized as "unprofitable friends." He proposed a course of study that began with histories that were "easy to read and truly worth the effort"—the *Tso Commentary, Records of the Historian,* and *History of the Former Han*—and then turned to the Six Classics.[56] For his countrymen this meant reading unpunctuated texts, that is, texts that had not been punctuated to be read as Japanese. Sorai was convinced that "if one can handle a punctuated text, one can handle an unpunctuated one. It is only a matter of the eye's being used to the unfortunate practice [of reading punctuated texts] that keeps one from reading unpunctuated ones. With hard work, these habits can be changed."[57] But this was only the beginning. One also had to learn to write in classical Chinese and actually compose poetry and prose compositions in that language, using the best classical Chinese poetry and prose as models.[58] If one did all of this, then, and only then, he assured Mizuno and Hikita, "would the ancients' intentions be clear."[59]

Sorai recommended more than mastery of the "ancient language," however. He called as well for the study of ancient Chinese etiquette and ritual—what he termed "ceremonial forms" (C. *shih,* J. *koto*).[60] These "ceremonial forms" were the established patterns of conduct and ritual performance that Gentlemen (C. *chün-tzu,* J. *kunshi*) learned when they studied the decorum appropriate to certain social and ritual occasions and when they practiced the rudiments of the six classical arts—ritual, music, archery, horsemanship, calligraphy, and mathematics. Because gentlemen were expected to conform to these ceremonial forms when participating in social and ritual events and performing any of the six arts, they were considered the repository of propriety, the font of good form.[61] As Sorai describes them, the study, rehearsal, and mastery of both classical Chinese literature and etiquette were simply different facets of the same process: the recovery of the Way of the Sages and Early Kings.

56. Sorai, *Sorai sensei tōmonsho, NRI,* 6:188, 194.
57. Ibid., pp. 188–189.
58. Ibid., pp. 179–180.
59. Ibid., p. 190.
60. I translate *koto* (C. *shih*) as "ceremonial form" because this is close to what Sorai appears to have meant when he used the word. See note 78 in the translation.
61. Sorai, *Benmei, NST,* 36:250, 253; Sorai, "Sui Shindō ni kaesu," *NST,* 36:512–513.

This effort to recover classical Chinese civilization had another dimension. It was the highest form of reverence one could show to the creators of this civilization—the Sages, Early Kings, and, of course, Heaven. Indeed Sorai's confidence in classical Chinese civilization in turn rested on his belief in a sentient Heaven, another recurring theme. This was not so remarkable in his day, as the belief in a sentient and omnipotent heaven—though a vestige of an earlier world-view—was still widespread. Like so many of his contemporaries, Sorai stood in awe of Heaven and believed that it alone understood the seemingly mysterious and unfathomable workings of nature.[62] He was convinced, too, that Heaven controlled human affairs and had intervened time and again in his own life and was behind everything that had happened to him. It was Heaven, for example, that had chosen him as its "instrument" and had led him to the long-obscured meaning of the Chinese classics and thus the lost civilization of ancient China.[63] And it was Heaven that kept him alive, despite frequent periods of illness, "to work on the enterprise of the Early Kings and Confucius."[64]

Sorai's belief in a sentient and omnipotent Heaven was important for another reason: it underwrote his confidence in the Way of the Sages and Early Kings. Heaven had overseen the creation of classical Chinese civilization and thus imbued it with a universality it would otherwise have lacked. After all, it was Heaven that had equipped the Sages and Early Kings with an unmistakable brilliance, giving them a profound understanding of human emotion and the "principle of things." It was this understanding that enabled the Sages and Early Kings to create the various artifacts, ceremonies, customs, and institutions of classical China.[65] This is the reason that Sorai repeatedly exhorts Mizuno and Hikita to mind Heaven. Respect "Heaven's will," he tells them, and recognize that "in situations beyond the reach of human knowledge and power, one has no choice but to leave everything to Heaven's will."[66] Everything that one has—one's inheri-

---

62. Sagara Tōru, *Nihonjin no dentōteki rinrikan* (Tokyo: Risōsha, 1964), pp. 215–216.

63. Sorai, *Bendō, NST,* 36:200.

64. Sorai, "Kōkoku ni atau [10]," quoted in Hiraishi, *Ogyū Sorai nempukō,* p. 124.

65. Sorai, *Sorai sensei tōmonsho, NRI,* 6:150.

66. Ibid., p. 157.

tance, one's good fortune, even one's nature—is "Heaven's work."[67] Sorai's frequent reminders about heeding Heaven point to still another theme that runs through his later writings.

Sorai's neoclassicism and belief in heaven, however, would have seemed hopelessly archaic and implausible had it not been for his vitalistic cosmology. Sorai saw change, unceasing change, as the fundamental trait of nature and human affairs and described "heaven and earth as dynamic phenomena" whose operations were "divinely mysterious" and beyond the ken of humans.[68] "Humans are active beings," he wrote in his fourteenth letter, "and thus when they are given things to do, talent and knowledge that had not been apparent may emerge."[69] "Not even snakes, scorpions, and poisonous insects are denied the transformative and nourishing powers of heaven and earth."[70]

Sorai did not invent this vitalistic discourse. It was part of the conceptual vocabulary available in his day. Itō Jinsai had advanced a vitalistic cosmology that Sorai admired.[71] It was also a prominent feature of that variant of the Neo-Confucianism imported to Japan in the 1500s which stressed the external and physical worlds and highlighted the operations of material force.[72] And these vitalistic cosmologies, as Sorai knew only too well, could be found in classical works such as the Book of Changes and Taoist texts and had been revived by Sung Confucian thinkers like Chang Tsai (1020–1077). In any event, Sorai appropriated this vitalistic discourse, inflecting it in his own way and working it into nearly everything he wrote in the 1710s and 1720s.

It was this dynamism that made Sorai's pedagogy and his proposals for reform so plausible. He was certain, for example, that anyone "would be changed naturally" who studied classical Chinese in the way he prescribed—namely, by looking only at unpunctuated prose

67. Ibid., pp. 157, 170, 175.
68. Ibid., pp. 153, 158.
69. Ibid., p. 166.
70. Ibid., p. 160.
71. Sorai, Ken'en zuihitsu, in Ogyū Sorai zenshū, edited by Imanaka Kanshi and Naramoto Tatsuya (Tokyo: Kawade Shobō, 1973), 1:466 (hereafter cited as KOSZ).
72. See Mary Evelyn Tucker, Moral and Spiritual Cultivation in Japanese Neo-Confucianism: The Life and Thought of Kaibara Ekken (1630–1714) (Albany: State University of New York Press, 1989), pp. 4–5, 11.

texts written before the end of the Han dynasty or poetry composed before the Sung and by actually writing prose and poetry that mimicked these models.[73] Such was the "mysterious functioning" of the Sages' pedagogy.[74] Although he was thinking of the ruling warrior class when he offered this advice, Sorai believed that the general population could be transformed as well. The trick was to get them to conform to the new behavioral norms. If this were done, regardless of whether they understood or agreed with these norms, "popular custom would be modified naturally; people's views would be corrected; and order would prevail in the provinces and realm. With these changes in prevailing customs, moreover, people would broaden their perspectives and realize their talent and virtue. Such is the mysterious functioning of the Way of the Sages and their pedagogy."[75]

Sorai and His Interpreters

Modern scholars have been unanimous in their recognition of Sorai's importance, and this was true from the outset. One of the first, if not the first, to argue for his significance was the Meiji journalist Yamaji Aizan (1864–1917).[76] He was followed by the pioneering historian of Japanese thought Inoue Tetsujirō (1855–1944), who devoted an entire volume of his three-volume study of Tokugawa thought to what he called the "ancient learning group" (J. kogakuha), which included Yamaga Sokō and Itō Jinsai as well as Sorai.[77] There was then a succession of Taishō (1912–1926) and Shōwa (1926–1989) scholars who shared this positive assessment. Despite this consensus, however, modern scholars have not agreed on why Sorai should be so highly regarded and what exactly constitutes his importance. They can be divided into three groups.

The first are those who have situated Sorai in the context of East Asian thought, particularly Confucianism, and assessed him in these terms. Typical in this regard are Yasui Shōtarō and Yoshikawa Kōjirō, who were impressed, among other things, by Sorai's linguistic

---

73. Sorai, *Sorai sensei tōmonsho, NRI,* 6:189–190.
74. Ibid., p. 190.
75. Ibid.
76. Yamaji Aizan, *Ogyū Sorai* (Tokyo: Minyūsha, 1896).
77. Inoue, *Nihon kogakuha no tetsugaku.*

achievements.[78] They pointed out that Sorai, and his precursor Itō Jinsai, were among the first Japanese Confucians who could not only read classical Chinese but also compose prose and poetry in impressively correct classical Chinese. Bitō Masahide has argued that Sorai, together with Jinsai and Yamaga Sokō, were the first Japanese scholars to confront Confucian texts in the way that Dōgen, Shinran, and Nichiren had confronted Buddhist texts centuries earlier. Minamoto Ryōen, echoing Bitō, has described the ancient learning movement as the product of the same process of naturalization that resulted in new varieties of Buddhism in the Kamakura period.[79] And Miyake Masahiko and Imanaka Kanshi attempted to locate Sorai in the Chinese philosophical context in order to show which ideas he borrowed from Chinese philosophers.[80] From this perspective, Imanaka argued for the novelty of some of Sorai's ideas—particularly his conception of human nature as fundamentally unchangeable, which, he suggested, was not only original in the larger Confucian context but may even have carried Sorai beyond the bounds of Confucian discourse.[81]

In the 1970s scholars, inspired by the work of Abe Yoshio, pointed out that the ancient learning thinkers seemed to replicate developments in continental Neo-Confucianism and thus might be seen as an outgrowth of Chinese and Korean Neo-Confucianism.[82] William Theodore deBary, the chief proponent of this view in the West, has described Sorai, Jinsai, and Sokō as merely rehearsing issues that had already been discussed on the continent and availing themselves of "certain options available in the Neo-Confucian system."[83] For deBary the significance of the new ancient learning discourse lies,

78. Yasui Shōtarō, *Nihon jugakushi* (Tokyo: Fuzambō, 1939), p. 150; Yoshikawa Kōjirō, "Jinsai-Tōgai gakuan," *NST,* 33:571–572.

79. Bitō Masahide, "Kokkashugi sokei toshite no Sorai," in *Nihon no meicho,* vol. 16: *Ogyū Sorai,* edited by Bitō Masahide (Tokyo: Chūō Kōronsha, 1974), pp. 53–54; Minamoto Ryōen, *Tokugawa shisō shoshi* (Tokyo: Chūō Kōronsha, 1974), p. 53. See also Kate Wildman Nakai, "The Naturalization of Confucianism in Tokugawa Japan: The Problem of Sinicization," *Harvard Journal of Asiatic Studies* 40(1980):157–199.

80. Miyake Masahiko, "Jinsaigaku no keisei," *Shirin* 48(1965):1–52; Miyake, "Itō Jinsai to sō-gen-min no jusho," *Nihon rekishi* 222(1966):61–78; and Imanaka, *Soraigaku no kisoteki kenkyū.*

81. Ibid., pp. 144, 186, 201–203; Imanaka, "Soraigaku no keisei to chūgoku shisō," *Shirin* 47(1964):210–211.

82. Abe, *Nihon shushigaku to chōsen,* pp. 493–496, 528–531.

83. DeBary and Bloom, *Principle and Practicality,* p. 167.

first, in the "notable continuity in the development of later Neo-Confucian thought" that it represents; second, in its being "a further extension of the original Neo-Confucian trend away from Buddhism"; and, finally, in the attention that its thinkers paid to the same problems that late Ming thinkers grappled with—for example, the "attention to the social and cultural contexts of 'real learning'" and a "compelling need for dealing with political and economic problems that were not susceptible of moralistic and spiritual solutions."[84]

A second group of scholars regards Sorai and the other ancient learning thinkers as quintessentially "modern." Maruyama Masao's *Studies in the Intellectual History of Tokugawa Japan (Nihon seiji shisōshi kenkyū)* is the classic statement of this view.[85] In this highly influential study of the ancient learning and national learning (J. *kokugaku*) movements, Maruyama characterizes Sorai, Jinsai, and Sokō as Japan's first "modern thinkers." His assessment is based on his conception of their collective intellectual achievement—namely, their destruction of Neo-Confucianism and of what he describes as the unity of nature and morality in the "Chu Hsi system." Maruyama has argued that the process began with Sokō, who separated human nature from morality. Jinsai, in turn, liberated the all-important concept of the way from both nature and human nature. And Sorai, building on the work of his predecessors, widened the separation of "norm" and "nature" by, first, mystifying Chu Hsi's conception of a rational Heaven and thus "transforming [Sung Confucian rationalism] . . . into its antithesis, irrationalism" and, second, by defining the "essence" of the Way of the Sages and Early Kings as centering on the task of governing the domain and the realm and thus as preeminently political. By doing this, Sorai denied Chu Hsi's claim that the personal morality of rulers and governments was linked and thereby enabled a "discovery of politics" that Maruyama regards as modern.[86]

Others have described the "modernity" of the new ancient learning discourse in somewhat different terms. Minamoto Ryōen has offered an assessment of Sorai that locates his writings in the tradition of what he calls *jitsugaku*, "real" or "practical learning." In *The Lineage*

84. Ibid., pp. 174–175, 177.
85. Maruyama's *Nihon seiji shisōshi kenkyū* has been translated into English by Mikiso Hane as *Studies in the Intellectual History of Tokugawa Japan* (Tokyo/Princeton: University of Tokyo Press/Princeton University Press, 1974).
86. Ibid., pp. 45, 50, 55–56, 81, 92.

of Tokugawa Rationalist Thought (Tokugawa gōri shisō no keifū),
Minamoto contends that Sorai's literary archaism—his "study of
ancient literary styles and forms" (J. *kobunjigaku*)—was "a revolution in the history of . . . *jitsugaku.*" Why? Because it offered what he
describes as "an empirical experiential science based on a perception
of reality that was liberated from value judgments and free."[87] Hino
Tatsuo, in *The Sorai School—From Confucianism to Literature (Sorai
gakuha—jugaku kara bungaku e),* has offered still another vision of
Sorai's modernity. In Hino's eyes, Sorai's great achievement was literary: he liberated literature from the confines of a restrictive Confucian
morality. "Confucians before Sorai," he writes, "wrote poetic and
prose compositions merely as a way of passing the time and were
wary of those who found positive value in the literary enterprise.
Sorai's promotion of the creation of poetic and prose compositions,
when considered in literary historical terms, thus has an epoch-mak-
ing significance, providing as it does a basis for a literary practice that
was independent of moral concerns."[88]

What is striking about the views of those who argue for Sorai's
"modernity"—Maruyama, Minamoto, Hino, and others—is that they
all use the same conceptual language. To cite the most obvious example, when they describe Sorai as loosening the strictures of an oppres-
sively moralistic Confucianism and enabling the emergence of new
ideas and practices—whether philosophical, political, or literary—
they situate him in a linear scheme in which movement from the
medieval to the modern, from the religious to the scientific, is a given
and positively regarded. Obviously this construction owes much to
the metanarratives that have dominated intellectual life in Europe,
the United States, and Japan since the mid-nineteenth century and
rehearses the particular "story" that they tell.[89]

87. Minamoto Ryōen, *Tokugawa gōri shisō no keifū* (Tokyo: Chūō Kōronsha,
1972), p. 90.
88. Hino Tatsuo, *Sorai gakuha—jugaku kara bungaku e* (Tokyo: Chikuma
Shobō, 1975), pp. 7–18.
89. This analysis of the conceptual language of those who stress the "modernity" of the ancient learning thinkers owes much to the work of Hayden White
and Louis Mink. See White, *Metahistory* (Baltimore: Johns Hopkins University
Press, 1973) and *Tropics of Discourse* (Baltimore: Johns Hopkins University
Press, 1978); and Mink, "Narrative Form as a Cognitive Instrument," in *The
Writing of History,* edited by Robert H. Canary and Henry Kozicki (Madison:
University of Wisconsin Press, 1978), pp. 129–149.

In the late 1970s and through the 1980s, a third group of scholars who had misgivings about these metanarratives began to explore other ways to interpret Sorai and other ancient learning thinkers. Inspired by the work of continental European theorists and historians, Harry Harootunian and Tetsuo Najita, the best known of these revisionists, suggested that the new ancient learning discourse be seen in broad spatial rather than linear terms as signaling the displacement of a highly influential Neo-Confucian discourse by other and competing discursive schemes. In his ground-breaking essay "Ideology as Conflict," Harootunian describes this change as "a profound epistemological break" based on a new recognition of "difference":

> Eighteenth-century writers turned their sights toward distinctions and discriminations in a general effort to establish the identities of things. No longer were connections and identities inevitable. Here, discrimination imposed upon comparison as its main method the recognition of the primacy of difference. This comparative technique was used increasingly by a variety of writers, from the most formal philosophic types to those anonymous scribes who drafted peasant petitions; comparison was often expressed in terms of management and calculability (J. *hakaru*) and the establishment of an orderly series of things. Measurement presupposed starting from a whole and dividing it into parts. Yet it was the parts themselves that observers were to equate with the whole; order, in its turn, established elements, the simplest that could be found, to arrange differences according to the smallest degrees.[90]

Harootunian makes two other observations about this change. First, it was an attempt, he writes, "to explain the world in a modality of contiguity, so as to accommodate the apparent differences among phenomena, not continuity, which had previously been made possible by a paradigmatic model of knowledge. Contiguity called forth the model of the syntagm, spatial relationships, and the categories of order, measurement, calculation, oppositions, and discrimination."[91] And it also relied on a "metonymic strategy" that enabled one "to establish part/whole relationships in an apprehension of the world in which one thing—the part—is reduced to another or is substituted for

---

90. Harry Harootunian, "Ideology as Conflict," in *Conflict in Modern Japanese History: The Neglected Tradition*, edited by Tetsuo Najita and Victor Koschmann (Princeton: Princeton University Press, 1982), p. 32.

91. Ibid., p. 31.

the whole. In this epistemological scheme, parts of presumed totalities functioned to construct a series of attributes (the whole) that could reveal the web of relationships that bound entities together. Metonymy promised to make sense of things that appeared to be different by relating them to each other in contiguity. Scholarship and action proceeded under the sanction of wholes made up of discrete parts."[92] Harootunian sees Sorai as the first of a series of thinkers who were responsible for this dramatic change, which in time would prove to be revolutionary.[93]

Tetsuo Najita echoes Harootunian in his important *Visions of Virtue in Tokugawa Japan: The Kaitokudō, Merchant Academy of Osaka*. He locates Sorai and Jinsai in the context of what he describes as a wide-ranging epistemological debate under way in the eighteenth century between those who saw "nature" as the ultimate source of knowledge and those who turned instead to "history." Najita places Sorai in the latter group, together with Jinsai and Sorai's disciple Dazai Shundai. Interestingly, Najita sees Jinsai's achievement as the most impressive. He credits Jinsai with creating a moral philosophy that affirmed the place and importance of merchants and providing, together with Nishikawa Joken (1648–1724), "a consistent philosophical affirmation of 'life' as 'virtue'," which enabled merchant action in the world and explains their emergence at a later date as political actors.[94]

The Texts

For this translation I have relied on the versions of *Sorai sensei tōmonsho* found in the Mizusu edition of *Ogyū Sorai zenshū, Nihon koten bungaku taikei,* and *Nihon rinri ihen* and found very helpful Bitō Masahide's modern Japanese rendering in the *Nihon no meichō*

92. Ibid., p. 32.

93. Ibid., pp. 31–38. This argument is developed more fully in Harootunian's *Things Seen and Unseen: Discourse and Ideology in Tokugawa Nativism* (Chicago: University of Chicago Press, 1988).

94. Tetsuo Najita, *Visions of Virtue in Tokugawa Japan: The Kaitokudō, Merchant Academy of Osaka* (Chicago: University of Chicago Press, 1987), pp. 10–11, 18–19, 24–29, 32–43; see also Najita, "History and Nature in Eighteenth-Century Tokugawa Thought," in *The Cambridge History of Japan*, vol. 4: *Early Modern Japan*, edited by John Whitney Hall (Cambridge: Cambridge University Press, 1991), pp. 596–659.

series. Although I have not seen them myself, the letters that Sorai sent to Mizuno and Hikita survive and are housed in the Tsuruoka Municipal Museum in Yamagata prefecture. Apparently they differ slightly from all other versions, whether copied or published, and thus are invaluable. Three versions are worth mentioning. The first is a handwritten copy in the possession of Ogyū Keiichi, a descendant of Sorai, which may very well be in Sorai's own handwriting.[95] The second is the first published edition, which appeared initially in Kyoto and then in Edo in 1727. The Kyoto edition was published by Noda Yahei and the Edo edition by Noda Tahei.[96] The modern annotated edition that appears in *Nihon koten bungaku taikei* is based on this edition. A later version in the Keio University Library dated 1734 is actually a commentary on *Responsals* written by Hanbe Ansu, whom Shimada Kenji describes as "a follower of Yamazaki Ansai's Shinto theories." Hanbe comments on each of Sorai's letters and appends a short critique as well.[97]

The publication history of *Master Sorai's Responsals* accounts for these several versions. The letters were not published in their original form but were lightly edited by two of Sorai's disciples: Nemoto Sonshi, who had transcribed them for Sorai and kept the copies that enabled their publication, and Hattori Nankaku, who proofread the final version.[98] This collaboration was fortunate, as Nankaku was the most gifted writer in Sorai's school and Sonshi, who had superb editorial skills, had already prepared authoritative editions of several of the Confucian classics under the auspices of the Ashikaga school.[99] But it does mean that the published version of the letters diverges slightly from the originals.[100] The changes appear to have been made while readying the letters for publication, and most are minor. For example, particles were changed, the orthography corrected, and the diction refined. In only two or three places was the meaning of sentences significantly altered, and these are indicated in the notes.

95. Shimada, "Kaidai-hanrei," *MOSZ*, 1:626.
96. Nakamura, "Kaidai," *NKBT*, 94:27.
97. Shimada, "Kaidai-hanrei," *MOSZ*, 1:629–630.
98. Ibid., p. 620.
99. Hiraishi, *Ogyū Sorai nempukō*, p. 123; Nakamura, "Kaidai," *NKBT*, 94:26.
100. Hiraishi, *Ogyū Sorai nempukō*, p. 162; Hino, "Hattori Nankaku denkō (ge)," *Ōsaka joshi daigaku kiyō—joshidai bungaku* 24(1973):26.

Master Sorai's Responsals

Way of the Gentleman

1. I received your request for advice about things that would be beneficial. Although you live in a distant province, I truly feel the intensity of your interest. The Way of the Sages is a broad, great, and infinite affair. If I were to describe the way of the Gentleman, I would say that nothing is more important than Humanity (C. *jen,* J. *jin*). Most people interpret Humanity as "Compassion" (C. *tz'u-pei,* J. *jihi*), but this is not the best rendering, as there are many kinds of compassion. The Sung Confucians' theory of heavenly principle and human desires dates from later times and diverges dramatically from the original meaning of the phrase as it appears in the classics.[1] In the *Mencius,* there is the saying, "The feeling of commiseration is humanity," but this has a par-

1. See also Sorai's last letter (no. 35) and his letters to Miura Chikkei, Yabu Shin'an, and Asaka Tanpaku, *NST,* 36:503, 508, and 538. The words "heavenly principle" (C. *t'ien-li,* J. *tenri*) and "human desire" (C. *jen-yu,* J. *jinyoku*) occur in the "Records of Music" chapter of the *Book of Rites:*

> Now there is no end of the things by which man is affected; and when his likings and dislikings are not subject to regulation (from within), he is changed into the nature of things as they come before him; that is, he stifles the voice of *heavenly principle* within, and gives the utmost indulgence to the *desires by which men may be possessed.* On this we have the rebellious and deceitful heart, with licentious and violent disorder. The strong press upon the weak; the many are cruel to the few; the knowing impose upon the dull; the bold make it bitter for the timid; the diseased are not nursed; the old and young, orphans and solitaries are neglected—such is the great disorder that ensues.

See James Legge, trans., *Li Chi: Book of Rites* (New York: University Books, 1967), p. 96; the italics are mine. Chu Hsi made much of these two terms and construed them as a dichotomy. See the preface to *Chung-yung chang-chü,* his commentary on the *Doctrine of the Mean.*

35

ticular context.[2] Inasmuch as the words "feeling of commiseration" are generally thought to refer to the compassion of nuns, they would be difficult to use today. In the *Book of Odes* is the phrase "the father and mother of the people."[3] This is the best gloss for Humanity.

How should one understand "father and mother of the people"? First, you should realize that fathers and mothers are the masters of the household. If one were to speak of the masters of poor households, there is, in these households, the difficult old mother-in-law, good-for-nothing wives, the happy-go-lucky eldest son and the naughty third son, and the newly married daughters-in-law. Among the hereditary retainers, there are the old and useless disabled servants. There are young servants, raised in the household from infancy and indulged by the master's kindness, who ignore what they are told to do. Yet to try to bring order to this chaotic household by means of right and wrong would not only be impossible but also unacceptable. The help in the household were inherited from Heaven and cannot be dismissed.

He who would be master of this household should look after all of its members. This means putting up with the summer heat, braving rain and thunder, cultivating the fields, cutting the grass, performing difficult tasks, enduring resentment, watching over the household,

---

2. *Meng-tzu,* IIA:6. The original passage reads: "The feeling of commiseration is the beginning of humanity." See Wing-tsit Chan, *A Source Book in Chinese Philosophy* (Princeton: Princeton University Press, 1967), p. 65.

3. *Shih-ching,* III:2. Sorai is referring to the following poem:

> Far off at that wayside pool we draw;
> Ladle there and pour out here,
> And with it we can steam our rice.
> All happiness to our lord,
> *Father and mother of his people.*

> Far off at that wayside pool we draw;
> Ladle there and pour out here,
> And with it we can rinse our earthen bowls.
> All happiness to our lord,
> Refuge of his people.

> Far off at that wayside pool we draw;
> Ladle there and pour out here,
> And with it we can rinse our lacquer bowls.
> All happiness to our lord,
> Support of his people.

See Arthur Waley, trans., *The Book of Songs* (New York: Grove Press, 1960), p. 182; the italics are mine.

and passing the time. Although one should scold and beat one's underlings from time to time and not show much compassion, one should not abandon them. Isn't worrying for a whole lifetime about one's underlings the natural inclination of fathers and mothers? The lower classes understand this. Why is this feeling of compassion lacking among warriors who receive one or two hundred *koku* or even one thousand, two thousand, or three thousand *koku*, and among lords of domains, those august personages who govern the realm? This makes them vastly inferior to lowly farmers, which is truly regrettable. If you were to ask why this is so, I would answer that it comes from the broadness or narrowness of a person's wisdom. When it comes to humble farmers, they all are like this. When it comes to warriors and lords, they worry—as we say—about their houses and domains.

If warriors and lords do not see their households and domainal populations as a family whose members should not be abandoned or cut off, it is because they have narrow concerns and can barely fulfill their own responsibilities and because their power prevents them from carrying out their duties. Thus, the largeness or smallness of a person's capacity is like the situation of the powerful and the powerless: if the powerless do a poor imitation of the powerful, then do you really believe that a person with narrow concerns can become a person of breadth and vision? Ordering a low-ranking retainer to worry about a domain or the country is tantamount to asking him to do what is both inappropriate to his status and impossible—namely, to become a person of broad vision. That warriors worry about their houses, lords their domains, and the Son of Heaven the realm are fortuitous things that are ultimately a gift from Heaven. Each has a particular destiny and thus a station in life, and there is nothing unusual about this. If people are unable to fulfill their responsibilities, it is because they have been influenced by bad habits and care little about their constituents.

Because the Way of Yao, Shun, and Confucius is not practiced in our society, Buddhists and Taoist groups urge people to ignore others and cleanse their own minds. These groups do this to calm—if only for a time—the raging controversies over right and wrong, vulgarity and correctness. Confucians of narrow vision regard Buddhism and Taoism as mysterious ways and imitate them, and their view that the Way of the Sages is nothing more than self-cultivation is spreading. As the shogun and the lords study these views, their perspectives gradually have narrowed. In the last hundred years, people have started to put their own convenience first, as can be seen in the growing practice of hiring migrant workers as servants. Consequently, both lords and servants are content to see this relationship as temporary, which has colored their view of everything else. These servants, for their part, are not at all concerned about their relatives, nor do retainers bother themselves with their lord's affairs. They think only of themselves, and today they serve up-to-date people. So if the recipients of Heaven's favor ignore the good fortune that Heaven has bestowed on them, it will surely disappear, which would be the height of wastefulness.

Be mindful of the phrase "the father and mother of the people." When actually put into practice, things will naturally accord with the Way of the Sages. As in Confucius' "there is one single thread binding my way together," the phrase "father and mother of the people" may not be exactly right, but it is probably not far off the mark.[4]

2. I understand your concern that the phrase "father and mother of the people," though fitting for governing one's subjects, is less suitable for serving one's superiors and for other things.[5] It may be impolite for me to say this, but your brightness allows you to bandy theory about. But I doubt that you have thought very deeply about this. Were you to continue in this way, you would be fine and live out your life as someone known to be bright. You would not progress in your studies, however. Once again, it is impolite for me to say this, but I think this would be unfortunate.

When moved to make inquiries from your distant province, you take what should be reflected on and without giving it much thought simply adopt what you agree with and express your reservations about the rest. Your coming right out and stating your doubts about what seems unreasonable to you is the result, ultimately, of your rely-

4. *Lun-yü*, IV:15. The entire passage reads: "The Master said, 'Ts'an! *There is one single thread binding my way together.*' Tseng Tzu assented. After the Master had gone out, the disciples asked, 'What did he mean?' Tseng Tzu said, 'The way of the Master consists in doing one's best and in using oneself as a measure to gauge others. That is all.'" See D. C. Lau, trans., *Confucius: The Analects* (Middlesex, England: Penguin Books, 1974), p. 74; the italics are mine.

5. Here I follow the version of this sentence that appears in the *Nihon rinri ihen* edition. See NRI, 6:149. A different version of this sentence appears in *Ogyū Sorai zenshū* and *Nihon koten bungaku taikei*. See MOSZ, 1:428, and NKBT, 94:185.

ing on your own knowledge and experience as a standard. Therefore, no matter what I say, it will not change what you have learned and experienced up to now, and this is why I am not responding.

Way of the Sages and Early Kings

3. I now see what you have been getting at in your last two or three letters. Everything you have studied up to now is a hindrance, and I suspect that you have not understood my reading of "the father and mother of the people." The point I tried to make in my first letter was that owing to the mistakes Confucians have been making for several hundred years, you have difficulty understanding what I am saying. For this reason, I would like to begin with the fundamentals.

Yao, Shun, Yu, T'ang, Wen, and Wu are called the ancient Sages.[6] All were rulers in ancient times. What is called the "Way" is the way that these Sages created for governing the realm and the country. The idea that the Way is the "way of heaven, earth, and nature" first appeared in the theories of Lao-tzu and Chuang-tzu and is not found in Confucian writings.[7] The Sages, with their broad and deep knowledge, created what they did in accord with human feeling and the principle of things, and as a result there was nothing unreasonable in their creations.[8] Today the prevailing theory is that the Way existed as

6. In his writings, Sorai speaks of eleven sages: Fu Hsi, Shen Nung, Huang Ti, Yao, Shun, Yu, T'ang, Wen, Wu, the Duke of Chou, and Confucius. He grouped them by generation: Fu Hsi, Shen Nung, and Huang Ti comprising the first; Yao and Shun the second; Yu, Kings T'ang, Wen, and Wu, and the Duke of Chou the third; and Confucius the fourth. See Sorai, *Sorai sensei tōmonsho, NRI,* 6:150, 187, 197–198; *Benmei, NST,* 36:218; *Bendō, NST,* 36:201.

7. Lao-tzu and Chuang-tzu are conventionally regarded as the founders of the ancient Chinese philosophical school known as Taoism, literally, the "school of Tao." Both are thought to have lived in the fourth century B.C. and left texts known by their names: *Lao-tzu* (also called the *Tao-te ching*) and *Chuang-tzu.* They called for a return to a "way" (C. *tao,* J. *michi*) that they described as absolute, constant, and universal and identified with the way things are naturally. Sorai has their conception of the way in mind here.

8. Sorai insisted on the universality of the way created by the Sages and Early Kings. As he saw it, this universality had two sources. First, the Sages and Early Kings understood the regularities in both nature and human affairs that careful study always revealed; second, they also understood human emotion—"emotion" (C. *ch'ing,* J. *nasake*) and "human emotions" (J. *ninjō*)—which were universal phenomena, bound by neither time nor space and thus the same in his day as they were in ancient China. See Sorai, *Benmei, NST,* 36:250.

a part of heaven, earth, and nature even before the Sages emerged, and if people seek the Way by returning to their own minds, they will discover that this view is mistaken.[9]

Inasmuch as it is a way that the ancient rulers created to pacify and govern the realm and country, one makes Humanity its foundation. Accordingly, it is because things are not seen in terms of the Humane Mind that your way of thinking about the Way of the Sages is different. This has happened because people have forgotten the Sages' original intentions. Because a knight's service to his lord is a means of helping the ruler govern the realm and country, if one does not begin by considering the words "father and mother of the people," then the duties of each office will go unfulfilled.

When one goes hawking, for instance, one person handles the hawks, another the dogs. The dog handlers regard the dogs as their responsibility and thus do not worry about the hawks. It is precisely because they forget that their dogs have to work with the hawks that they fail to fulfill their responsibilities.

In the education of children, there are proctors who continually scold them and proctors who side with them. The scolding proctors affect a formidable pose, but they do not really dislike the children; they want only to make sure the children pay attention to their lessons. The sympathetic proctors, who seem to be the childrens' allies, are, in fact, merely assisting the scolding proctors. And so although both sets of proctors have different tasks, each understands the other's intentions. It is like *kyōgen:* only when the *shite* and *waki* are in step does the play work.[10]

Thus it is clear that if the way of vassals does not know the way of rulers, their understanding will be different. It is not just this, however.

9. See also letters 33 and 35. Sorai was consistently critical of the Neo-Confucians' description of the way as "natural" (C. *tzu-jan,* J. *shizen*). Chu Hsi, for example, wrote "The way is the nature of heaven and principle" and "The way is the path of nature." See Chu Hsi, *Meng-tzu chi-chu,* 2A, and *Chung-yung chang-chü,* 43b.

10. *Kyōgen* is a type of comic drama that dates from the eighth century and may be Chinese in origin. In the medieval period, it developed side by side with another, somewhat more somber, dramatic form, *nō,* although at this stage both were popular forms of entertainment. From the late fourteenth century, they enjoyed the patronage of the military aristocracy, including the Ashikaga shoguns; at this point *kyōgen* and *nō* became somewhat more distinct, and *kyōgen's* identity as a comic form was firmly established. *Nō* plays normally use only two actors: a lead actor *(shite)* and a supporting actor *(waki).*

The division of everything in the world into four classes—warriors, peasants, artisans, and merchants—is something that the Sages devised long ago; the four classes of people did not exist naturally in heaven and on earth.[11] Farmers cultivate the fields and feed the people of the world. Artisans make household goods for the people of the world to use. Merchants keep produce and goods circulating and thus benefit the people of the world. And the warriors oversee all of this and prevent disorder. Although each class performs its own duties, each assists the others, and so if any one class were lacking, the country would be the worse for it. And so because people live together, they all are officials helping the ruler become the "father and mother of the people."[12] Seen in this way, things should be clear. This is why knights are called "gentlemen." As for the word "gentleman" (C. *chün-tzu* J. *kunshi*), *shi* is a general term for "man" and refers to a man with a ruler's virtue. When Confucius said, "The gentleman who ever parts company with Humanity does not fulfill that name," he was pointing out that the word "gentleman" originated in Humanity.[13]

In the way of Chuang-tzu and Lao-tzu, one lives a hermit's existence deep in mountain forests. Buddha, too, abandoned society, left his family, and became a beggar. His path is based on his own experiences and thus centers on matters pertaining to the individual mind and ignores the issue of governing the country and realm. This is the reason we can regard as a remnant of Buddhism and Taoism the theory that the Way of the Sages is concerned exclusively with governing one's own mind and that if one's own mind is governed, then the realm and country will be governed naturally.

The Way of the Sages has its own conception of self-cultivation. It

11. See letters 33 and 35. Sorai may be thinking of Hayashi Razan's repeated assertions that the social order corresponds to the natural order, a view widely held by Japanese Confucians through the seventeenth century. Sorai insisted that institutions are human creations, or "artifice" (C. *tso-wei*, J. *sakui*), as he put it, and not natural phenomena—that is, "in heaven and earth and in nature" (C. *t'ien-ti tzu-jan*, J. *tenchi shizen*). See Sorai, *Benmei, NST*, 36:216–218, 220–221, 250.

12. There is a significant variation here. The word *morosugi*, which I translate as "living together," does not occur in all versions of the text. In the *Nihon rinri ihen* edition, for example, the word *monosuki*, "eccentric" or "selfish," appears in its place. I agree with the editors of the Mizusu edition that *morosugi* makes more sense here. See Sorai, *Sorai sensei tōmonsho, MOSZ*, 1:430.

13. *Lun-yü*, IV:6. See Arthur Waley, *The Analects of Confucius* (New York: Vintage Books, 1938), p. 103. I have altered Waley's translation slightly.

says that if a ruler's personal behavior is improper, his subjects will be resentful and resist. Therefore, rulers who want their subjects to submit must cultivate themselves and govern the realm and country. This is the essence of the Way of the Sages. For example, no matter how much one regulates one's mind and refines one's person and no matter whether one is as polished as the most perfect gem, if one is not attentive to the people's concerns and livelihood and if one does not know how to govern the country, what difference will all this make? Thus, if one does not see things in terms of "the father and mother of the people," no matter how beautiful or persuasive one's language is, what one does will be as different as clouds and mud and ten thousand miles from the way of Yao, Shun, Yu, T'ang, Wen, Wu, and the Duke of Chou as transmitted by Confucius. You should recognize that this is precisely where the Way of the Sages and the way of the Buddhists and Taoists diverge. You should reflect on this.

Learning

4. With my last letter, you indicated that your doubts about the issues you raised at the outset have disappeared and that other questions have been answered as well. This is wonderful! As your scholarly achievements grow over the years, your doubts will multiply, and this will be proof of your profiting from our exchanges. I admire your determination. Generally speaking, scholarship is something one comes to understand on one's own. All of Confucius' teachings were of this sort, and pedagogies like this exist even in decadent ages. With the lecturing pedagogies that are popular today, one takes what was simplified for the purposes of the lecture and uses it for everything and thus has no doubts and learns very little.[14] If you do this for some

14. Sorai was critical of the pedagogies used at other Confucian schools, especially lecturing. He had two criticisms. First, he noted: "Lectures have a fixed method: one reads the Four Books and Chu Hsi's *Reflections on Things at Hand* (Chin-ssu lu) in a certain order," and no attention is paid to the individual student. Second, lectures are too abstract, and the knowledge they convey is too superficial, too easily grasped, and too quickly lost. Sorai favored the pedagogy used by the Sages, one that "instructed by means of performances (J. *waza*) and not simply principles. Although teachers can certainly espouse principles, what they present are really fragments, and they have to wait for students to understand the material on their own. The reason is that when theory is used to instruct students, it offers the shallowest kind of knowledge and is not very useful. As with all things, if one does not do it on one's own, one can never know it." See Sorai, *Taiheisaku, NST,* 36:455–456.

time, your thinking will become rigid, and this can do incalculable harm. In the end, people come to believe that the Way of the Sages is far removed from human emotions and not at all suitable for contemporary society. But because the knowledge of the Sages is the highest knowledge, people should understand that the Way of the Sages is suitable for any age. If they think in this way, then a multitude of doubts should emerge once again.

5. I understand that you have been reading history, and I think this is commendable. You indicated that you are reading Chu Hsi's *Outline and Digest of the Great Mirror.* If you read history, *The General Mirror for Aid in Government* is good.[15] It is, however, a rambling work that seems to go on forever and is not easy to read. So when you read it, you should consult a catalog. The word *"kang"* in the title—*The Outline and Digest of the Great Mirror*—means "catalog," and the word *"mu"* refers to the original text. And so although the *Outline and Digest* does not differ appreciably from the *Great Mirror,* the latter's style is not that of a catalog. Moreover, because the *Outline and Digest* was written with words of praise and blame, it immediately conjures up a theory, and if you read it, your scholarship will become theoretical in the way that Chu Hsi's is. This, I think, would be unfortunate.

Vulgar scholars will tell you to use the *Outline and Digest* to grasp principle, but this is not "real learning."[16] Remembering the reputations of the successive generations of historical figures mentioned in the *Outline and Digest* and evaluating them accordingly are nothing more than rote memorization and mere gossip. But because the per-

---

Sorai proposed that students study and actually practice classical Chinese literary styles and forms of ritual and etiquette. They were to "imitate" (C. *fang-hsiao,* J. *hōkō*) and "practice" (C. *hsi,* J. *narau*) these models until they had mastered the "particulars" and achieved what Sorai called "concrete form" (C. *wu,* J. *mono*), which is discussed more fully in note 152. For more on Tokugawa pedagogies, see Richard Rubinger, *Private Academies of Tokugawa Japan* (Princeton: Princeton University Press, 1982), pp. 43, 49, 53.

15. *The General Mirror for Aid in Government (Shih-chih t'ung-chien)* was written by Ssu-ma Kuang (1019–1086) in the style of the classic *Tso Commentary.* It is an account of the 1,362 years from the end of the Chou dynasty (1122/1027–221 B.C.) through the Later Chou dynasty (A.D. 557–581). Chu Hsi wrote *The Outline and Digest of the Great Mirror (Shih-chih t'ung-chien kang-mu)* as a commentary on Ssu-ma Kuang's work.

16. Sorai uses several different terms to refer to Neo-Confucians and their ideas: "Sung Confucians," "Sung learning," "latter-day scholars," "later generations," "vulgar scholars," and "philosophy of principle."

petuation of popular gossip is considered learning, even those of good
character, when they engage in learning of this sort, often turn out for
the worse. Such are the baneful effects of the Chu Hsi style of philosophy of principle.

When one reads *The Outline and Digest of the Great Mirror,* there
is not one appealing person in the past or present. Since readers of
this text thus see their contemporaries in this light, it is not surprising
that human character is deteriorating. Moreover, the arguments presented in the *Outline and Digest* are like woodblock printing: the
form is set; the principle is fixed; the method of argumentation is pre-
determined. Heaven, earth, and people are dynamic phenomena, and
to view them as though they were bound and tied with rope is truly a
useless kind of learning and merely encourages glibness. It is for this
reason that the factual *General Mirror for Aid in Government* is far
superior to *The Outline and Digest of the Great Mirror.* If one is
seduced by Chu Hsi's pernicious theories in his commentaries on the
Four Books and his *Reflections on Things at Hand* and then reads the
Outline and Digest, one will be imposing Chu Hsi's view on the past
and present and simply mastering his theories.[17]

Learning is what Hsün-tzu called "the way of flying ears and long
eyes."[18] Furthermore, understanding the affairs of foreign countries
that one, as a resident of this country, has never seen is like sprouting
wings on one's ears and flying. Being born in the present world but
knowing what happened many millennia ago as though one saw them

---

17. Chu Hsi not only wrote commentaries on what came to be known as the
Four Books—the *Analects, Mencius, Great Learning,* and *Doctrine of the Mean*—
but he also was responsible for the grouping of these four texts and their reception
as the core of the Neo-Confucian canon. Before he did this, however, the *Great
Learning* and *Doctrine of the Mean* were chapters in the *Book of Rites (Li-chi).*
The *Reflection on Things at Hand (Chin-ssu lu)* is an anthology of Neo-Confucian
writings that he, together with Lü Tsu-ch'ien (1137–1181), compiled in 1175–
1176. It includes the writings and sayings of Chou Tun-i (1017–1073), Chang Tsai
(1020–1077), Ch'eng Hao (1032–1085), and Ch'eng I (1033–1107).

18. Sorai has misattributed the phrase "the way of flying ears and long eyes." It
is from the "Nine Defenses" chapter of the *Kuan-tzu* and not from the *Hsün-tzu.*
The original passage reads:

> First, lengthen your ears;
> second, fly your eyes;
> third, plant your brilliance—
>> brilliance knows what lies beyond a thousand miles and with the
>> subtle and unseen.

with one's own eyes is what is meant by "long eyes." Thus, seeing and hearing a variety of things and being true to what actually exists constitute what is called learning, and this is why learning achieves its ultimate form in history.

Not being conversant with the past and present and Japan and China is tantamount to seeing things in terms of our own contemporary customs, and this is truly like being the veritable "frog in a well."[19] In our time, an ordinary person who is not accomplished will not be of much use. Those who might be called accomplished are to be found among the elderly, and those who have visited many domains are especially valuable. But those without learning are limited by their age and thus are unaware of things that took place more than fifty or sixty years ago. No matter how many provinces a person has seen, he will not know the whole country. With this I think you get my point.

You may read the classics, but your ignorance of historical reality means that you will see the age of the Sages as you do the present and thus make many errors. When one hears the words of unlettered military theorists, one realizes that they believe Minamoto Yoritomo resembled present-day shoguns and that Chichibu Shigetada and Wada Yoshimori were like contemporary lords.[20] This is the result of their not knowing how ages differ. If one does not fully understand how provinces and ages have changed, one will not know that "the principles of order and disorder and prosperity and decline apply to the past and the present, nor will one know that the Sages created a

19. *Chuang-tzu*, Ch'iu-shui. This simile appears in the "Autumn Floods" chapter of the *Chuang-tzu*. The original passage reads:
Jo of the North Sea said, "You can't discuss the ocean with a well frog—he's limited by the space he lives in. You can't discuss ice with a summer insect—he's bound to a single season. You can't discuss the Way with a cramped scholar—he's shackled by his doctrines. Now you have come out beyond your banks and borders and have seen the great sea—so you realize your own pettiness. From now on it will be possible to talk to you about the Great Principle.
See Burton Watson, trans., *The Complete Works of Chuang Tzu* (New York: Columbia University Press, 1968), pp. 175–176.
20. Minamoto Yoritomo (1147–1199) was designated shogun by Emperor Go-Toba in 1192 and established the first military government in Japanese history. Wada Yoshimori (1147–1213) figured in the Minamoto victories over their rivals, the Taira, and later was made head of the Board of Retainers (J. *samurai dokoro*). He helped overthrow Yoritomo's successor, Yoriie, and brought to power another of Yoritomo's sons, Sanetomo. Chichibu Shigetada (dates unknown) was a warrior from the eminent Chichibu house, which claimed descent from Emperor Kammu (737–806).

way that was suitable even for ages in decline."[21] Inasmuch as history is composed of uncountable incidents and a multitude of characters, the expansion of one's knowledge and experience will be without end. This is the value of studying history.

Among the various histories, the *Records of the Historian* and the *Tso Commentary* are the work of fine historians.[22] They recorded events in such a way that readers feel they are seeing them with their own eyes, and they not only find the account interesting but also are drawn to the heart of the event and moved. This is the value of these histories. The antiquity of these texts gives them the flavor of ancient learning, and they have the added value of not having fallen into the trap of Sung-style learning. *The General Mirror for Aid in Government* surpasses *The Outline and Digest of the Great Mirror,* but its unfelicitous style keeps readers from being drawn into the heart of an event and moved. As books are hard to find in the provinces, no matter what you read, you will need to travel widely and keep studying the past and present. If you avoid theory and read widely, you will be sure to benefit.

6. I understand that you have read the political writings of various T'ang and Sung Confucians. Because reality is best understood on its own terms, this is wonderful!

There is something you should understand about this. The era of the Three Dynasties was an age of feudalism. The period after the Ch'in and Han dynasties and up through the T'ang, Sung, and Ming dynasties was an age of commanderies and prefectures.[23] Ages of feu-

21. See letters 12 and 19. Sorai discerned a recurring pattern in history as dynasties rose, prospered, deteriorated, and fell. He called this pattern the "way of order and disorder, prosperity and decline" and sometimes the "way of order and disorder." See Sorai, *Taiheisaku, NST,* 36:458.

22. *The Records of the Historian (Shih-chi)* is a monumental work of 130 chapters that ranges from prehistory to the reign of the sixth ruler of the Han dynasty, Emperor Wu (r. 140–87 B.C.). The project was conceived and begun by Ssu-ma T'an, a Grand Historian at the Han court, and completed by his son and successor, Ssu-ma Ch'ien (145–90 B.C.). It served as a model for East Asian historical writing well into the twentieth century. One of the earliest extant Chinese histories, the *Tso Commentary (Tso-ch'uan)* narrates in thirty volumes the major political, military, and diplomatic events that occurred between 722 and 468 B.C. in the various feudal states that comprised China at this time. It has been attributed to a certain Tso Ch'iu-ming, about whom nothing is known.

23. The three dynasties were Hsia (2205–1766 B.C.), Shang (1766–1122/1027 B.C.), and Chou (1122/1027–221 B.C.). Sorai mentions the succeeding dynasties as well: Ch'in (221–207 B.C.), Han (207 B.C.–A.D. 220), T'ang (618–906), Sung (960–1279), and Ming (1368–1644).

dalism and ages of commanderies and counties have very different institutions and laws.[24] In feudal societies, the realm is divided up among lords, and the Son of Heaven rarely governs directly. Vassals of these lords have stipends and hold their fiefs from generation to generation. Although some worthy individuals are hired, social status is fixed: knights are always knights and lords are always lords; for this reason, people's minds are settled and society is calm. Laws and regulations are rudimentary at best, and the people are governed by means of feelings of gratitude and obligation, with priority given to instilling a sense of shame. Both lords and knights regard the provinces and commanderies as their own and govern them accordingly.

In the world of commanderies and counties, there are no lords, and knights are knights for only one generation. Knights, moreover, are not given fiefs but receive rice stipends, and meager ones at that. They take on large numbers of underlings and gain prestige in this way. The commandery and county heads who govern the provinces of the realm are like our intendants: they are transferred every three years, and their authority is weak. Their way of establishing laws and regulations differs from that of the Three Dynasties; their laws and regulations are strict and complicated.[25] Governors and county heads manage the provinces and commanderies on behalf of the Son of Heaven and are moved every three years, and so it is customary for them to be preoccupied with quickly proving their effectiveness. Because farmers have risen to become prime minister, it is widely believed that knights should seek to advance themselves. This is the great difference between the Three Dynasties and later ages.

In ancient times Japan, too, had commanderies and counties, but the

24. Commanderies (C. *chün*, J. *gun*) and counties (C. *hsien*, J. *ken*) were the basic administrative units of the Chinese imperial state. The state of Wei first used the commandery in 400 B.C. and the state of Ch'u devised the county in 588 B.C. Ch'in adopted both institutions and used them in the imperial state it created in 221 B.C.

25. The intendants (J. *daikan*) were officials dispatched to the countryside by the Tokugawa and various domainal governments. They oversaw the payment of taxes, maintained order, and settled disputes in the area of their jurisdiction. Strictly speaking, only those responsible for territories whose productive capacity was less than ten thousand *koku* were called *daikan;* those with territories larger than ten thousand *koku* were called *gundai.*

country is now divided into feudal domains. This is why much in the writings of T'ang and Sung Confucians would be hard to adopt.[26] Moreover, many of their proposals exist only on paper. One might think that their recommendations are reasonable, yet even things that are hard to implement seem plausible at first glance. The writers of these proposals were interested solely in showing off their talent and knowledge, cared little about actuality, and hoped that what they wrote sounded good. Because these books are the work of scholars, everything will seem reasonable when you read them. Yet this is not the case.

Ruling a country is like a physician controlling an illness. Let us suppose a patient is lethargic; has phlegm, a fever, and indigestion; suffers from lumbago; is coughing and troubled by diarrhea. Skillfully mixing various medicines that will restore this patient's vital force, reduce the phlegm and fever, eliminate the indigestion, suppress the lumbago, stop the cough, and halt the diarrhea may seem a reasonable treatment, and in fact this is what unskilled doctors do. A skillful doctor, however, first restores the patient's vital force and then takes steps to control the phlegm and fever. Although some treatments first eliminate phlegm and fever and then restore the vital force, simply restoring the vital force obviates the need to pay attention to anything else, and the various other ills will disappear naturally. If lumbago is diagnosed as the original ailment and controlled, the rest will heal naturally. But because lumbago is a long-term ailment, if it is treated but not controlled the patient might recover naturally anyway. Some doctors adhere to the practice of dealing speedily with superficial symptoms and stopping the diarrhea and then and only then undertaking a permanent cure. And when it comes to effecting cures, there is no single method that all skilled practitioners use. Amateurs believe it is best to consider each thing in detail, and the Japanese and Chinese are alike in this way.

This is why writers, to convince their readers, advance empty theories that they cannot detail. It happens that readers sometimes regard as reasonable what the writer knows is a fabrication. When Ssu-ma Ni asked Confucius about the meaning of his saying "The gentleman's words are reasonable," Confucius answered: "Carrying them out is difficult." That is, it is difficult for a gentleman to govern a

26. Sorai is reminding his readers that the political and economic institutions of the seventh and eighth centuries were modeled on the centralized Sui and T'ang imperial states but later were displaced by feudal institutions.

country and pacify the people, and for this reason a gentleman who has mastered the art of governing does not speak of it lightly or simplistically.[27] This is the essence of Confucius' statements. There are many political theories that, as a popular proverb puts it, "go on and on about what cannot be done." Administrative methods are best thought of as administrative methods, and one usually cannot understand methods of governing a country solely by reading classical texts. Thus, reading texts on political economy to broaden your knowledge is a species of learning: learning is a matter of simply taking everything in and broadening one's knowledge. However, your finding the various political theories interesting and wanting to use them right away in your own administration, I am afraid, will not be very productive. It is precisely because one's worldview is narrow that unextraordinary things seem extraordinary and because one's capacity is limited that one wants to apply and use what one knows right away. This is shortsighted and is the sort of thing that the young do. This warning is important.

The Mandate of Heaven

7. The issue of insufficient courage, which you raised, is an understandable concern for a military house. In the Way of the Sages, Wisdom, Humanity, and Courage were called the three universal virtues, and gentlemen were expected to have courage.[28] Generally, one is wary of the unknown and careful with the unfamiliar—this is a psychological constant.[29] A ship captain's not fearing the wind and waves

27. *Lun-yü*, XII:3. Sorai altered the original passage, changing its subject from the "humane person" (C. *jen-ch'e*, J. *jinja*) to the "gentleman" (C. *chün-tzu*, J. *kunshi*). Compare Sorai's "The gentleman's words are reasonable" with the original's "The humane person's words are reasonable." He may be conflating this passage with II:13: "Tzu-kung asked about the gentleman. The Master said, 'He puts his words into action before allowing his words to follow his action.'" See Lau, *Confucius: The Analects*, p. 64.

28. *Chung-yung*, XX. The original passage reads: "Wisdom, humanity and courage, these three are the universal virtues. The way by which they are practiced is one." See Chan, *A Source Book in Chinese Philosophy*, p. 105. Here I follow Chan in rendering *chih/chi*, *jen/jin*, and *yung/yu* as "wisdom," "humanity," and "courage."

29. Sorai refers often to *ninjō no jō*, literally the "constants of emotion," which I render as "psychological constants." He believed these were universal emotions that disposed people to do certain things and not others. See letters 9, 12, 13, 16, 19, 22, and 29 and Sorai, *Benmei, NST*, 36:242 for more on the emotions.

may seem like courage, for example, but put him on a horse and he will be terrified. When those whom society regards as great warriors find themselves in situations in which they must know ritual procedures, they cower because these are matters about which they know nothing and to which they are not accustomed. At night children are afraid of the fields where they play during the day, because they cannot see very much in the dark. When one knows principle, however, none of these things is frightening. When one merely wants to know principle but does not, the more one knows, the more doubts one will have, and the more careful one will be. My first point, then, is that courage is simply a matter of getting used to something.

When people get used to what they merely tolerated at first, their caution and fear gradually disappear, because when they get used to something, they know it well. Accordingly, if people are afraid of what they are not used to, this does not mean that they lack courage. Although things are generally as I suggested earlier, there is much in the world that is beyond our ken and power. In these situations, courage always falters. In situations beyond the reach of human knowledge and power, one has no choice but to leave it all to the Mandate of Heaven. Thus the foundation of courage and cowardice rests on whether one knows or is ignorant of the Mandate of Heaven.

Most who have attained wealth and position foolishly believe that these achievements resulted from their own knowledge and effort. What they fail to realize is that all of this was due to Heaven's assistance. When one works, one succeeds; when one does not work, one gains nothing—all follow a single principle. In the end, however, there is no success without the assistance of the Heavenly Way. It is like farmers cultivating their fields. They may do their very best to cultivate their land, but storms and droughts remain beyond their control. Consider, too, the upbringing of wellborn children. Although the children of lords have wet nurses, are warned time and again not to do anything wrong or to get hurt, and never are allowed out of sight, sometimes even they fall into harm's way. The children of the poor, in contrast, have busy mothers and are poorly clothed, left out in the sun, soaked by rain, and free to roam and walk about at will. Although no one minds them, they grow up without tumbling into ditches or being kicked to death by cows or horses. People attribute their good fortune to the watchfulness of the god of children, and I believe that this is, in fact, the case. When people understand this, they realize that everything comes down to the Mandate of Heaven. When they understand the Mandate of Heaven, there is little that upsets them.

As for my explanation of the idea of "accumulating righteousness" in the *Mencius,* remember that Mencius had ulterior motives for saying this, and so you should regard it as a secondary matter.[30] In the practice of "accumulating righteousness," one is, unfortunately, strongly theoretical and single-minded. But when one abandons theory, one loses sight of what one was about to pursue and thus lacks courage. You should regard Confucius' "he who does not understand the will of heaven cannot be regarded as a gentleman" as evidence of his familiarity with the three virtues of Knowledge, Humanity, and Courage.[31] The Way of Yao, Shun, Yu, T'ang, Wen, Wu, the Duke of Chou, and Confucius recorded in the Six Classics is about the Mandate of Heaven.

8. Generally speaking, the winds, clouds, thunder, and rain are the mysterious operations of heaven and earth. Thunder, in particular, has the power to generate life.[32] This is all I know. From ancient times, there has been talk of the material force of yin and yang, the actions of ancestral and heavenly spirits, and the various kinds of animals thought to possess magical power.[33] Heaven and earth are active phenomena that are divinely mysterious and beyond our ken. We have contemplated these phenomena with our limited knowledge and generated the several theories presented earlier. Yet all of these are conjec-

30. *Meng-tzu,* IIA:2.

31. *Lun-yü,* XX:3; Waley, *Analects,* p. 233.

32. I translate *toku* (C. *te*) as "power," since Sorai uses it here in the way that the Taoists in the Eastern Chou (771–221 B.C.) did—as referring to a life-giving power or property. See Arthur Waley, *The Way and Its Power: A Study of the* Tao Te Ching *and Its Place in Chinese Thought* (Boston: Houghton Mifflin, 1935), pp. 31–32.

33. Sorai is describing an archaic Chinese worldview that saw spiritual beings (and what one scholar has called "mythical animals") controlling human affairs. This conception obviously originated in prehistory and survived into the Western Chou (1122/1027–771 B.C.). Sorai's reference to yin and yang is problematic, however, since these terms may not be truly archaic. They appear in the Eastern Chou (771–221 B.C.) and are identified with a certain Tsou Yen (305–240?), whose writings have not survived, and later became a staple in Han cosmology. See Kwang-chih Chang, *Art, Myth and Ritual in Ancient China* (Cambridge: Harvard University Press, 1983), pp. 56–80; Kwang-chih Chang, *Early Chinese Civilization* (Cambridge: Harvard University Press, 1976), pp. 180–184; and Chan, *A Source Book in Chinese Philosophy,* pp. 244–245.

ture; none is a sure thing. This being the case, all one can say is that what is called the learning of gentlemen involves studying the way of pacifying and governing the country, and human affairs is difficult enough.

Ever since the Sung Confucians misread the words "investigating things" and "extending knowledge," people have believed that learning requires that one determine everything from the disposition of the wind, clouds, thunder, and rain to the principle of every blade of grass and each tree.[34] When one examines the motives of those who do this, one discovers that they want to have contemplated everything in heaven and earth to the fullest possible extent, to know everything, and to become erudite. In the *Doctrine of the Mean,* there is mention of how "there are things which even sages do not know."[35] How can someone with only average intelligence know everything?

The Sung Confucians' theories push people to do what they cannot do, and consequently Confucians often speak of the shame they feel when they do not know something. This is sheer arrogance. There is nothing like this in the Way of the Sages and Worthies. Our ignorance extends beyond the wind, clouds, thunder, and rain, however. All the mysterious operations of heaven and earth exceed the reach of human

34. In his discussion of the phrases "investigating things" (C. *ke-wu,* J. *kaku-butsu*) and "extending knowledge" (C. *chih-chih,* J. *chichi*), which occur in the *Great Learning,* Sorai is attacking Neo-Confucian conceptions of learning. Sorai believed that learning required only that one study the Chinese classics, chiefly, the *Book of Odes* and the *Book of History.* See *Daigakukai,* his commentary on the *Great Learning,* in *Nihon meike shisho chūshaku zensho,* edited by Seki Giichirō (Tokyo: Ōtori Shuppan, 1973), vol. 1: *Gakuyō-bu ichi,* p. 3. *Nihon meike shisho chūshaku zensho* is hereafter cited as *NMSCZ.*

35. *Chung-yung,* XII. The original reads:
The Way of the superior man functions everywhere yet is hidden. Men and women of simple intelligence can share its knowledge; and yet in its utmost reaches, there is something which even the sage does not know. Men and women of simple intelligence can put it into practice; and yet in its utmost reaches there is something which even the sage is not able to put into practice. Great as heaven and earth are, men still find something in them with which to be dissatisfied. Thus with the Way of the superior man, if one speaks of its greatness, nothing in the world can contain it, and if one speaks of its smallness, nothing in the world can split it. The *Book of Odes* says, "The hawk flies up to heaven; the fishes leap in the deep." This means that the Way is clearly seen above and below. The Way of the superior man has its simple beginnings in the relation between man and woman, but in its utmost reaches, it is clearly seen in heaven and on earth.
See Chan, *A Source Book in Chinese Philosophy,* p. 100.

knowledge. What lies behind the blossoming and fruiting of grasses and trees, the rush of rivers, the soaring of mountains, the flight of birds, the scurrying of beasts, and the behavior and speech of humans is beyond our ken. The arguments of the scholars of the philosophy of principle rely heavily on the terms "yin" and "yang" and the "five elements," but all they have done is to construct a theory based on conjecture. Claiming to know something does not necessarily mean that one really knows it. The same is true with the way of governing the country as well; one never knows enough. What exists above a mysterious and unfathomable heaven and earth is fundamentally unknowable, which is why thunder should remain thunder.

9. You mentioned that you forced your parents to stop believing in Buddhism. This was because it was at odds with the prevailing conception of filial piety and thus seemed unconventional. Latter-day Confucians saw the Way of the Sages as their own private possession and blithely created their own schools. Mencius fought with Yang Chu and Mo-tzu; the Sung Confucians did battle with the Buddhists and Taoists.[36] Indeed, when one examines their attitudes, one discovers that they all were exceedingly jealous of one another and petty. As a great way that pacifies the country, the Way of the Sages cannot be compared with Buddhism and other doctrines. Buddhism teaches people to govern their own minds and thus does not hinder the Way of the Sages. Although Buddhists are a problem not worth considering, when one does confront them, one finds that they are what might be called "occupational enemies."[37] Given their Buddhist origins, it is hardly surprising that the Sung Confucians are critical of their own affinities to the Buddhists.

It is a real shame that you who have studied ancient learning, under the influence of the Sung Confucians, commit the unfilial act of prohibiting your parents' Buddhism. Remember that Confucius believed that playing draughts was better than being idle, because he recog-

---

36. Mo-tzu (fl. 479–438 B.C.) and Yang Chu (fl. 350 B.C.) were Chinese philosophers active in the fifth and fourth centuries B.C. Both are mentioned in the *Mencius*: Yang Chu is described as espousing an egoism summed up in the phrase "everyone for himself," and Mo-tzu is presented as the author of a doctrine of universal love. Virtually nothing is known about Yang Chu, and Mo-tzu's identity and occupation are still the subject of scholarly debate. The text that bears his name is a collection of his sayings recorded by his students. See *Meng-tzu*, IIIA:5, IIIB:9, VIIA:26.
37. The locus classicus of this term is unknown.

nized that people cannot simply do nothing.[38] The leisured are lonely and do all sorts of untoward things. Confucius' statement reveals the Sages' profound understanding of human emotion. If you can see the issue from this angle, governing the country and the realm should be like turning something over in the palm of your hand. As one ages, one stops working for others, loses interest in music and sex, and has fewer and fewer old and intimate friends and no young acquaintances. When household affairs have been entrusted to one's offspring, one no longer needs to be involved, and as a result one gradually gets lonelier and lonelier. Apart from playing *go,* chess, or *suguroku,*[39] visiting temples and going to hear sermons, and reciting the *nembutsu* at home, what is there to salve one's loneliness?[40] Should we not give some thought to the world of the elderly?

Buddhism has been practiced in the world for nearly a thousand years, and priests too are citizens of the realm. The Way of the Sages has the pacification of the general population as its foundation. With recurring illnesses like lumbago and spasms, even if one were treated by the famous Warring States physician Pien Ch'üeh, no blend of medicines could offer a cure.[41] Likewise, not even snakes, scorpions, and poisonous insects are denied the transformative and nourishing powers of heaven and earth. And so even Buddhism is valuable in an age of decline. I suspect that it is because you are given to distinguish-

---

38. *Lun-yü,* XVII:22. Although most modern scholars believe that Confucius refers to board games in this passage, there is no agreement about their exact nature.

39. *Go, shōgi,* and *suguroku* were popular board games in Sorai's time. Both *go* and *shōgi* are thought to have originated in India and to have reached Japan from China, where both games were also played. During the Tokugawa period, the government opened a special office to oversee *go* and *shōgi* competition, established official schools, and sponsored an annual tournament held at Edo Castle. Both games flourished under official sanction. *Suguroku,* a game that resembled backgammon, was introduced from China in the eighth century and was popular among the aristocracy. It was played in Sorai's time but went out of fashion in the latter half of the Tokugawa period.

40. "Reciting the *nembutsu*" was a Buddhist practice requiring one to utter the words *namu amida butsu* (I take my refuge in the Buddha Amida). One of several different kinds of *nembutsu* practice, it was introduced to Japan from China by the Tendai sect and taken up with great enthusiasm by the various Pure Land sects.

41. Pien Ch'üeh was a famous Chinese physician said to have been active in the fifth century B.C. and credited with writing *The Classic of Difficult Issues (Nanching),* which one modern scholar describes as "the classic of the medicine of systematic correspondences." See Paul U. Unschuld, *Nan-Ching: The Classic of Difficult Issues* (Berkeley and Los Angeles: University of.California Press, 1986), p. 3.

ing sharply between right and wrong, improper and proper, that you
have made this error. It is because I have benefited so much from your
kindness that I have stated my ideas with so little reserve.

Talent

10. I received your inquiries about political affairs, and I am not at
all sure that you have grasped the distinction between law and human
beings.[42] It is true, as you stated, that there are many good laws and
many unenforceable laws as well, and consequently all laws must be
closely examined. Yet most of those who discuss political affairs look
only at the merits and demerits of laws and make the mistake of not
knowing the Way. The *Book of Changes* says: "If you are not the right
person, the way cannot be realized."[43] People are far more important
than laws. A law may be bad, for example, but if the person enforcing
it is able, it will have some benefit. But if laws are merely examined
and never enforced and if those who enforce them are bad, laws will
not be of any use whatsoever. Moreover, laws vary according to the
people who carry them out. Laws are no longer examined as carefully
as were those of the Early Kings, and Wang Mang and Wang An-shih,
using the *Rites of Chou,* flooded the realm with their poison.[44] Inquir-

42. See letters 22, 24, and 31. The distinction between "humans" (C. *jen,* J.
hito) and "law" (C. *fa,* J. *hō*) was fundamental in Chinese political theory. The
interest in the humanity of those who ruled originates in Confucius' insistence that
the moral quality of rulers matters more than the techniques and devices used in
governing. See *Lun-yü,* II:3, XII:17, XIII:13. The emphasis on "law" was the hall-
mark of the Legalist school, which favored the use of rewards and punishments as
well as law. See *Han Fei-tzu,* Yu-t'u, Yang-ch'üan, Chien-chieh, Nan-mien, Wu-tu.
Both conceptions of government coexisted from the Han dynasty (207 B.C.–A.D.
220) onward and provided Chinese rulers, bureaucrats, and political thinkers with
a wide range of options. In the eleventh-century debates on government policy, for
example, there were those, like Hu Yüan (993–1059) and Sun Fu (992–1057),
who argued for moral solutions to the problems plaguing the government of the
day, and others, like Wang An-shih (1021–1086), who called for innovative institutional solutions to these problems. Sorai was well aware of this debate and conversant with the Confucian and Legalist vocabularies its disputants invoked.
43. *I-ching,* Hsi-tz'u ch'uan; Richard Wilhelm, trans., *The I Ching: Or Book of
Changes* (Princeton: Princeton University Press, 1950), p. 349.
44. Wang Mang (r. 9–23) and Wang An-shih were two of the most daring
reformers in Chinese history. The former, a relative of a reigning Han empress,
usurped the throne in A.D. 8 and carried out sweeping reforms designed to solve
the regime's fiscal problems. He strengthened government monopolies and commodity controls and debased the currency, but his most famous measures were the
abolition of slavery and the nationalization of the private estates that were siphon-

ing into political affairs without looking into personnel matters is like collecting the fabled methods of amateur physicians. No matter how fine the medicine, if the administering physician is unskilled, it will not cure the illness. Physicians may lack the amateurs' fabled methods, but if they are well trained, they will be able to cure the illness. Moreover, if one is not used to these fabled methods, they are hard to use. Sometimes a certain method cannot be used, owing to the physician's ability and personal inclinations, which is the reason the Sages and Worthies searched so assiduously for good people. Good people produce good laws. The reason you ignore personnel matters and are obsessed with laws is that you prefer to rely on your own talent and knowledge. But this is not a quality of great ministers. The saying "plain and sincere, without other abilities" closes the hundred chapters of the *Book of History,* and it seems that Confucius took some care with this.[45] I would like you to understand this issue. Your many years of generosity have allowed me to ignore your questions and turn your attention to other matters, and even to present my own foolish ideas.

11. In your last letter, you asked about the problem of not having any good people, and here I think you made a verbal slip. Because most people speak as you do when they have a little learning, it is natural that they think in this way. But this is just talk.

In our country, the cultivation of the five grains is the same now as it was in the past, and there has never been a problem fulfilling the world's needs at any time. The same is true with people. Although those who grew up with the instruction and nurture of the Sages and Worthies differ from those living in ages without these teachings, there is always usable human talent in any age. Are you thinking of "a country without people"?[46] This phrase refers to "a court's lacking talented

---

ing off tax money that should have gone to the state. Nearly eleven centuries later, Wang An-shih, chief councillor of the Sung state, carried out comparably dramatic reforms to improve state finances. He revived government price regulation and commodity controls, carried out land surveys and water control projects, and instituted a new tax system and a loan program for peasants. Sorai is critical of these reforms because they relied more on institutions and law than on human talent and were more Legalist than Confucian.

45. *Shu-ching,* Ch'in-shih pien; James Legge, trans., *The Chinese Classics* (Hong Kong: University of Hong Kong Press, 1960), vol. 3. *The Chinese Classics* is hereafter cited as *CC.*

46. I have not been able to locate the source of the phrase "a country without people."

individuals willing to serve," which results from the court's not employing them. It is understandable that in ages wanting in good people, the worthy and the talented sink into the lower ranks or are lost among the general population. Your account of "not having any good people" is like Mencius' anecdote about the king who blamed the deaths of his subjects on the harvest.[47] This is an affront to the Way of Heaven.

As I noted in my last letter, the trouble with your relying on your own ability and knowledge is that it blurs your vision, and talented people are never apparent to you. I infer from your letter that you believe that "human talent" should always meet your specifications and what does not is not "human talent." The Sung Confucians and others have a problem with issuing specifications. If you read Chu Hsi's *Outline and Digest of the Great Mirror*, you will see that there was not a single person in the realm, past or present, who was to his liking. Chu Hsi saw everyone as having some flaw. When I say, as I often do, that I cannot recommend that you read *Outline and Digest*, this is the reason. To issue your own specifications when searching for talented people is to establish your own preferences, and no one will fit them—no one in the entire realm or in the past, present, or future.

More specifically, "people's minds are as different as their faces."[48] That no one has a face like yours proves my point. Ask for the impossible, and no one will satisfy you, and your subordinates will flatter

47. *Meng-tzu*, IA:3. The original passage reads:
Now when food meant for human beings is so plentiful as to be thrown to dogs and pigs, you fail to realize that it is time for garnering, and when men drop dead from starvation by the wayside, you fail to realize that it is time for distribution. When people die, you simply say, "It is not me. It is the harvest that is to blame." In what way is that different from killing a man by running him through, while saying all the time, "It is not me. It is the weapon that is to blame." Stop putting the blame on the harvest and the people of the whole empire will come to you.
See Lau, *Mencius*, p. 53. I have modified this translation slightly.
48. *Tso-chuan*, Hsiang kung, 31. The phrase occurs in the following passage: "Tzu-chan said, 'People's minds are as different as their faces.'" See Legge, *CC*, V:562. Sorai was fond of this analogy and used it often. The idea that people were innately so different that universal standards of thought and behavior were unworkable and unduly constraining is central to his thinking about ethical and institutional matters, appearing in everything he wrote after 1711. See *Bendō*, *NST*, 36: 200, 203; *Benmei*, *NST*, 36:212, 240, 242, 244; *Gakusoku*, *NST*, 36:258; *Chūyōkai*, *NMSCZ*, 1:7, 44. It appears in his minor writings and correspondence as well. See "Kashushi o okuru jo," *Soraishū* (Edo, 1740), 10:14, and "Yabu Shin-an ni atau (7)," "Tōmon tsuki," and "Hori Keizan ni atau," *NST*, 36:508, 510, 530, 534.

you to become your favorite. The problems that plague our world come down to this. Think carefully about this.

12. You indicated that you are not a very good judge of people, and I see yours as a sincere request. Because you have admitted this frankly, I shall try to be specific. In my last letter, I said that you merely relied on your own preferences because true human talent was not apparent to you. You are certainly not the only one making this mistake. It is an unfortunate contemporary practice that encourages people always to be hiding things, with the result that the whole world exists as in a fog.

Think of the generals from the days when our country was young.[49] All had barely escaped death and endured hardship. They knew nothing about the way of order and disorder, prosperity and decline, but they did understand human emotion and social custom and cared little about the picayune things our contemporaries agonize over. Order and peace have prevailed for some time, and our country has been ruled by stipended men who have grown up with wealth, who have no awareness of human emotions or social customs, and who have had the most comfortable upbringing imaginable. They have come, gradually, to have the most delicate dispositions: they worry about trivialities and excessively upbraid their subordinates for their mistakes. Those who force their subordinates to be perfect are described today as good officials. This is why they worry about making mistakes and raise their children to be this way. This is now common practice. As a result, people do not become very involved with their work and worry chiefly about hiding things from their superiors. And it is precisely because people are so cautious that their talent does not appear.

You should listen to stories about the way things were in your ancestors' time. Every talented person who achieved fame at that time was what we would call eccentric. But this was not a problem, because at that time one did not hide anything and one's foibles were readily apparent. When eccentricity is apparent, so too is human talent. Nowadays those unsullied by the unfortunate social customs that are spreading are eccentric in many ways, and you should realize that without eccentricity there is no talent. In fact, you would do well to choose officials from among the eccentric. Selecting men who are not

49. Sorai is referring here to the late sixteenth and early seventeenth centuries in Japan.

eccentric and who already have developed talents is what I called in my earlier letter "specifying one's preferences."[50] You should see those without eccentricity as Mencius' "honest villagers," Confucius' "clever and pretentious talkers," or Hsün-tzu's "ordinary folk."[51]

13. You contend that eccentrics are hard to handle, and your misgivings are understandable. Being unfamiliar with the nature of human emotions and social customs, you worry about the damage that eccentrics might do; in fact, you are obsessed with this issue. You should realize that this is the result of your not being fully educated

50. Sorai himself was regarded as something of an eccentric. As he put it: "Having been raised in the country, I was a bumpkin who was not above saying to my lord's face what others could never bring themselves to say." His rural adolescence imbued him with other qualities that distinguished him from his colleagues in the Yanagisawa house: he laughed so heartily at official functions that he was asked to pipe down and felt so constrained by the punctilio of life in the Yanagisawa house that often, after attending an official function, he would dash home, strip off his clothes, and drink heavily. See Sorai, *Seidan, NST,* 36:289–290.

51. Here Sorai reveals his preference for eccentrics and contempt for conformists and braggarts. The term "honest villagers" (C. *hsiang yüan*) occurs in Confucius' discussion of those with whom a gentleman should associate. The "honest villagers" are condemned for their eagerness to please those around them and for lacking any true moral sense. Here is Mencius' description of "honest villagers":

If you want to censure them, you cannot find anything; if you want to find fault with them, you cannot find anything either. They share with others the practices of the day and are in harmony with the sordid world. They pursue such a policy and appear to be conscientious and faithful, and to show integrity in their conduct. They are liked by the multitude and are self-righteous. It is impossible to embark on the way of Yao and Shun with such people. This is why they are called "enemies of virtue."

See *Meng-tzu,* VIIB:37; Lau, *Mencius,* p. 203. I have altered Lau's translation slightly.

In all three places in the *Lun-yü* where the words "clever and pretentious talkers" (C. *ch'iao-yen ling-se*) occur, Confucius is issuing a stern warning about those who seem to have Humanity (C. *jen*) but in fact do not. See *Lun-yü,* I:3, V:25, and XVII:17.

"Ordinary folk" (C. *yung-jen*) were the least attractive of the five grades of people that Hsün-tzu discussed in the Lord Ai chapter (chap. 31):

Those who are unable to say good things; who do not know how troubled they are or how to select worthies and good knights and to entrust themselves to their care as a way of resolving their anxieties; who do not know how to apply themselves; who, when they are at rest, lack a foundation; who, when choosing things in their daily lives, do not know how to value them; and who are carried along by the flow of things and do not know where to return . . . . Those who fit this description can be called "ordinary folks."

See *Hsün-tzu,* Ai-kung pien; see also Jung-ju pien.

and lacking broad perspective. As long as you are unable to get past this barrier, you will never be able to govern the province.

An eccentric is like an unruly horse. As long as you fail to quiet it, you will be too nervous to mount it. This is natural. Even if you succeed in mounting this horse, you will sit there unsure that you have the means to control it. There will be stable hands and horse dealers who have no trouble mounting unruly steeds, but even they can hardly be said to have mastered every equestrian technique. Even if they had, it might not matter, as horses are active creatures and one never knows how wild they will be. Your problem is that you have a tendency to worry, and this may be why things are not going well. If you broke in an unruly horse, you would realize that there is no need to worry. Unless you are willing to be thrown many times, you will never be able to mount unruly steeds.

You observed that today people are given to scolding others for their failings and thus work at eliminating their own. They are convinced that they cannot afford to put eccentrics in the wrong positions, and they complain that eccentrics are hard to employ. If one is unwilling to be thrown, one will never be able to mount a horse. Similarly, if one is unwilling to make the mistake of putting eccentrics in the wrong positions, one will never be able to use their talent. You must realize that Yao did this when he put Kun in the wrong position and that the Duke of Chou erred with his brothers, Kuan Shu and Ts'ai Shu.[52] When one worries about appointing people to the wrong positions, one is thinking only of outdoing the Sages. This, you should realize, is a great misapprehension.

A successful physician sees gypsum and monkshood root as useful medicines, whereas an unskilled physician sees them as unreliable substances and searches, instead, for medicines that have the same effect but not their drawbacks.[53] Yet there has never been such a med-

52. Yao, who was conventionally regarded as a Sage, is said to have appointed Kun to stem the flooding that plagued the realm. Kun labored for nine years but failed to complete the task. The Duke of Chou, the brother of King Wu and one of the founders of the Chou dynasty, appointed his brothers Kuan Shu and Ts'ai Shu to oversee the conquered Shang territories, but they rebelled when he became the regent for the young crown prince, Ch'eng, who was too young in 1116 B.C. to succeed his father, King Wen.

53. Both gypsum (C. *shih-kao,* J. *sekkō*) and monkshood root (C. *fu-tzu,* J. *fushi*) were used by physicians in East Asia. Monkshood *(Aconitum napellus)* was a poisonous herb whose roots, when dried, were used as a sedative.

icine in the past or the present. If one uses substances like gypsum and monkshood root skillfully, one will not worry about their peculiarities. All medicines are toxic, but when used for their positive effects, they are not regarded as toxic. In my last letter, I spoke of "eccentrics," because this is the name that contemporary social custom has given to such people, and I wanted to discuss the issue in ways that you could understand. My point was that everything in heaven and earth has both positive and negative features and brings both profit and loss. When you make use of someone's positive qualities, because you don't really understand these qualities, you will see only their negative traits and see this person as eccentric; and this despite the fact that there is no such thing as a "discarded thing" or "discarded talent."[54] When employing people, therefore, one should use their positive qualities and overlook their negative ones; this is the Way of the Sages. Yet owing to the popularity of the heterodox theory that

54. See letters 12 and 14. The words "discarded things" (C. *ch'i-wu*, J. *kibutsu*) and "discarded talent" (C. *ch'i-ts'ai*, J. *kisai*) occur in Taoist works and reveal their acceptance of things as they are. "Discarded things" appears in chapter 27 of the *Tao-te ching*:

> Those who excel in traveling leave no wheel tracks;
> those who excel in speech make no slips;
> those who excel in reckoning use no counting rods;
> those who excel in shutting use no bolts yet what they have shut cannot
>   be opened;
> those who excel in tying use no cords yet what they have tied cannot be
>   undone;
> therefore the sage always excels in saving people, and so abandons no
>   one; always excels in saving things, and so *discards nothing*.
> This is called following one's discernment . . . .

See Lau, *Lao Tzu,* p. 84; the italics are mine. I have altered Lau's translation slightly.

The words "discarded talent" occur in a discussion of the importance of following "natural principles" in government in "The Art of Rulership" chapter of the *Huai Nan-tzu.* It reads:

> It is not as if the sage could possibly go against what natural principles make inevitable in accomplishing things or run contrary to what is natural in making the bent straight or the contracted outstretched! He always takes advantage of what a thing can be used for and uses it accordingly.

> Where concerted strength is applied,
>   no task is too great;
> where the intelligence of the people is engaged,
>   no undertaking will go unfinished.

one should transform one's physical nature and attain the comprehensive virtues of Centrality and Harmony, bad physicians are wont to heal illnesses by collecting dried orange peel and licorice root.[55]

14. You want to employ eccentrics in accordance with my theory, but people's strengths are not apparent to you, and you say, "Of course. This is not surprising." Because you have not had much practice, I would guess that you are not able to understand this. Are you aware of your own strengths? I would like to say a little more about this.

Generally speaking, this is something that you simply cannot know. I, for example, have no sense of my own strengths. Having cultivated and refined the way of learning since childhood, I take pride in what may be my only asset. I have not done many other things and thus am unaware of other assets I may have. I know that you are adept at handling official matters and that you know your way around the shogun's court. And when it comes to the work of warrior generals, aren't you a little like Kōsaka Toratsuna of old?[56] Or perhaps you

---

A deaf person can be made to chew the animal sinew
    used in covering bows, though he cannot be made to hear.
A dumb person can be made to work in the horse stables,
    though he cannot be made to speak.

This is because their physical persons are not whole and their abilities have their limitations.

That which has a specific form can occupy a position appropriate to it and that which has a specific ability can undertake a task appropriate to it.

When the strength of a person lifting a burden is equal to the task, he does not feel it too heavy to raise; when the ability of a person pursuing a task matches it, he feels no difficulty.

When everything large or small, long or short, finds its niche,
    then there is equality in the empire without anything being able in any
    way to surpass another.

Because the sage uses both big and small, long and short, there is no *discarded talent.*

See Roger Ames, *The Art of Rulership: A Study in Ancient Chinese Political Thought* (Honolulu: University of Hawaii Press, 1983), pp. 181–182; the italics are mine. I have altered Ames' translation very slightly.

55. Both dried orange peel (C. *ch'en-p'i,* J. *chinbi*) and licorice root (C. *kan-ts'ao,* J. *kansō*) were used by East Asian physicians.

56. Here I follow the *Nihon koten bungaku taiku* edition in substituting *inishie* for *migi.* See *NKBT,* 94:196. Kōsaka Toratsuna (1527–1578) was a warrior general skilled in military strategy and tactics who served Takeda Shingen (1521–1573) and distinguished himself in battle. He later wrote *Kōyō gunkan,* a military classic.

resemble Naitō Shūri?[57] Or do you have the strengths of a Yamagata or a Baba?[58] You cannot know much about this matter. With these examples, I think you get the gist of what I am saying.

Even if one wanted to gauge a person's talent, ability, knowledge, and wisdom, simply watching that individual for a whole day and praising and criticizing him will not enable one to say that one knows his strengths, although diviners, physiognomists, and spiritualists could do this. Humans are active beings, and thus when they are given things to do, talent and knowledge that had not been apparent may emerge. Without putting people to work, even the Sages would have difficulty knowing whether they had talent and wisdom. Hence the saying in the *Book of History* that "he does such and such a thing" is suggesting that one should actually put people to work.[59] If one thinks that one can first discern a person's strengths and then hire him, one will not be able to make good use of that person. You should realize that people who are not actually employed remain unknown entities.

Moreover, when employing people, one should follow certain procedures. If one insists on giving them instructions and ordering them about, people will never get involved in their work, with the result that their full talent and ability will not emerge. Furthermore, if one does not permit these employees to make small mistakes, even though one has not given them instructions, they will not be very devoted to their appointed tasks. This is why unless one actually puts them to work, one cannot know them. And if one does not leave matters to them, one is not truly employing them. These are enduring principles, and there is no mysterious way outside this; it is the Way that the ancient Sages transmitted. You should not have the slightest doubts about any of this.

Military Preparedness

15. You asked about military preparedness. Military science is the province of the president of the Board of War, as described in the *Rites*

---

57. Naitō Shūri was a vassal of Takeda Shingen, who is mentioned in the military classic, *Kōyō gunkan*.
58. Yamagata Masakage was a vassal of Takeda Shingen and held a castle in Ejiri in Suruga province. The Baba were vassals of the Takeda, as well, and here Sorai is thinking of Baba Nobuharu. Both Masakage and Nobuharu were killed on 29 June 1575 at the Battle of Nagashino.
59. *Shu-ching*, Kao-yao pien; Legge, CC, III:71.

of Chou, and is one part of the Way of the Sages that should be clarified.[60] The methods of drawing out the enemy, advancing and deploying an army, and defending a castle are what Japanese military theorists discuss, and their theories usually conform to the customs of their own province. Although there are things about their theories that I find unpersuasive, these are secondary. Consider, for example, the feints one uses in battle. Most of what Japanese military theorists say is a recapitulation of past battles or worked out on living room floors in peacetime. You should regard these theories as useless, empty doctrines.

One's first concern should be Humane Government—for without the unity of rulers and their subjects, military victory is impossible. Thus the lord of a province should regard his warriors and the general population as a family that has been given him by Heaven, a family that he cannot abandon. He should make their hardships his hardships and do what he can to make them enjoy their lives in the province. You should regard this as the cardinal principle of military science.

The very first thing the lord should do to lessen the hardships of warriors and the general population is to locate them in the countryside, divide them into bands, and appoint leaders who will keep them together. In the past, all warriors lived on fiefs in the countryside, but at some point they congregated in the castle towns and, as a result, turned into aristocrats. Castle towns are like inns; consequently there are many expenses, and the financial situation of warriors has gradually worsened.[61]

The interior of the province is now public domain. Warriors are no longer permitted to wander freely through the province, for when they do they frequently break the law. One consequence of this policy

60. The *Rites of Chou (Chou-li)* has been described as a Confucian manual on ritual and etiquette. It dates from the third or fourth century B.C. and is one of three such texts that survive to the present—the others are the *Book of Rites (Li-chi)* and the *Book of Etiquette and Ceremonial (Yi-li).* The version that survives is largely the work of Han scholars.

61. In 1646, the Tokugawa abandoned the practice of subinfeudation in their own territories and began to move their warriors from the countryside to the nearby castle towns and in some cases the capital, Edo. Seven years later the Tokugawa ordered the lords of domains that had not done this to do so, and most complied. Sorai saw this migration of warriors to cities and castle towns as one of the sources of the myriad problems of his day. His solution, of course, was to resettle the warriors and much of the urban population in the countryside. For a full discussion of Sorai's resettlement plan, see *Taiheisaku, NST,* 36:478–479, and *Seidan, NST,* 36:299–300.

is that warriors are not familiar with the geography of their own province or with the affairs of the population at large. And thus even when they become magistrates and officials, they know nothing about their subjects' situation. Because low-ranking warriors no longer live on fiefs, their dealings with farmers are little more than battles over who taxes and who is taxed, and no feelings of obligation bind them to each other; in fact, warriors and farmers see each other as enemies. If warriors lived on fiefs, feelings of obligation would unite them with the farming population; the farmers would become their retainers; both rulers and subjects in that province would be as one. If a captain were designated, then suits and water disputes would be resolved locally and there would always be someone familiar with local conditions. And by building granaries, amassing surpluses, and preparing for emergencies—for the benefit of both warriors and the population at large—hard times would not mean suffering.[62]

The general population is dumb and does only what they are used to doing. This being so, one must plan even everyday matters, grow grasses and trees locally, carry out the annual tree cutting at New Year's, assemble the hundred craftsmen, and encourage commerce. If the root (read agriculture) is slighted and the branch (read commerce) is favored, the province will decline, and the resulting mob of merchants will become the bane of the province.[63] But there are cases in which a poor province became rich through its merchants. In any event, one should pay attention to the ebb and flow of commerce. Because extravagance and gambling signal the deterioration of the population at large, one should prohibit gambling, using harsh punishments to enforce the prohibition, and set up a system regulating dress and housewares. If you are cautious, your province should become as wealthy as you want. Here it is absolutely crucial to keep the general population of the province from leaving.[64] Moreover,

62. Sorai's confidence that warriors, once resettled in the countryside, would "be one" with the rural population may originate in his memories of his family's sojourn in Kazusa, where they lived for over a decade during their banishment from Edo. They apparently got along well with the local population and were treated generously, perhaps because Sorai's father was an eminent physician.

63. Here Sorai rehearses a staple of Confucian statecraft—namely, that agriculture is primary and commerce secondary.

64. Sorai is alluding to Mencius' discussion of what rulers must do to keep their subjects from leaving and to attract those who would come. See *Meng-tzu*, IIA:5, IVA:9.

teaching people to be candid and honest and fostering a sense of shame are the true way of war. Archery, horsemanship, spear handling, and fencing are not what rulers should encourage.

Administering and Taxing Provinces

16. As you observed in your letter, military preparedness is the foundation of a province. Those who have jurisdiction over provinces and commanderies are entrusted with this land by their ruler, and thus their first concern is ensuring that it is not taken by others. In ancient times, the Son of Heaven was called "ten thousand axles"; lords were called "thousand axles"; nobles and high officials were "hundred axles." Using military allotments as designations is done for the same reason.[65]

In the legal codes of the Han dynasty (207 B.C.–A.D. 220), the statutes governing thievery are placed at the beginning and are seen as comparable to rebellion. This is because achieving a state of military preparedness sufficient to suppress thievery was an urgent matter. When order and peace prevail, military authority is used to quiet the people; when there are outbreaks of thievery, there must be military means to suppress them immediately.

Although present-day intendants are the district magistrates of old, they are not only not equipped militarily, but they are also unwilling to be responsible for pacifying the areas under their jurisdiction. Rather, they regard the collection of the annual revenue as their most important task. They appoint to official positions very low-ranking warriors who can read and do sums, and thus their occupational status is low, and they naturally become petty. These are tasks even corrupt officials can perform. Although this does not apply to the lords of fiefs with only ten thousand to thirty thousand *koku* who have small domains and few troops, lords with seventy or eighty thousand *koku* fiefs have intendants who must be given military support. Owing to the demands of what is known in our time as the "crop inspection system," only the small-minded are willing to become intendants.[66]

With regard to tribute and taxation systems, the fixed-tax method is

65. *Meng-tzu*, IIA:2.
66. The crop inspection system (J. *kemi*) was a form of taxation used during the latter half of the Muromachi (1336–1573) and through the Tokugawa (1600–1867) periods. In this system, the agricultural yield of each plot of land was estimated annually and a fixed portion was then paid to the authorities.

the best.[67] During the Three Dynasties, the Hsia used the tribute system, the Shang instituted the well-field system, and the Chou employed the tithing system. The tithing system is implicit in the tribute and well-field systems. The well-field system distinguishes between public and private fields and therefore is difficult to use in later ages. The tribute system has fixed tax rates. The great Yu established it, and it is the best method of taxation. The Sages had a deep understanding of human emotions and created this method of taxation on the basis of their insights into conditions in the past and present. The so-called crop inspection system has led to various abuses and improprieties among officials. If one instituted constant rates, the path to self-aggrandizement would be blocked, and, although one had done nothing to prevent the abuses and improprieties associated with the crop inspection system, the improprieties would disappear naturally. The fixed-tax system was used in ancient Japan and in China from the Ch'in and Han to the Yüan and Ming dynasties.

Notice that using crop inspections to determine tax rates means that a province's wealth goes directly into the pockets of officials. If one used the fixed-rate system, one would collect set amounts with which one would regulate the province's finances, and the latter would be simple. If the *torika* system were converted into a fixed-rate system, anyone could serve as an intendant.[68] Because those who govern regard intendancies as lowly positions, it is hard to appoint warriors from high-ranking families—as a result, high-ranking officials become estranged from the general population and are like wooden dolls. You should regard all existing institutions as a legacy from the Warring States period and as mere stopgap measures.

Profit

17. Although your idea that, generally speaking, profit should be a priority and that attention should be paid solely to the circulation of

---

67. The fixed-tax method (J. *jōmen*) was adopted in 1721 to correct the shortcomings of the crop inspection method. It levied a fixed tax rate on agricultural production—a tax rate determined by averaging tax payments over the preceding five, ten, or twenty years. A similar method of taxation was used in medieval times as well.

68. *Torika* referred to the portion of the tax yield taken by the lord of a domain.

currency and goods sounds exceedingly fine, it diverges from the great Way of the Sages and Early Kings. Making profit a priority and eliminating all obstacles to circulation may seem, for a time, to be prudent; but because these are not profound and farsighted conceptions, they ultimately will do much harm to the Way. How this will turn out, if implemented, is not clear. You should realize that these seem to be brilliant ideas but in fact are the height of stupidity. Those who are preoccupied with the circulation of currency and goods are controlled by merchants. Circulation is second nature to merchants and is the way of those with that occupational status—which is why even lords, with all their power, are no match for merchants. This being so, you should realize that if one is preoccupied with circulation, financial power will certainly fall into the hands of merchants—all as a result of your seeking immediate profit. I think you need to give this question more careful consideration.

Loyalty

18. The idea that our bodies belong to our lords and are no longer ours is popular nowadays. Yet this idea does not appear in the Way of the Sages and should be seen as the stuff of flattery and sycophancy. Even the Sung Confucians misconstrue the word "loyalty" and gloss it in this way. "Loyalty" is seeing another person's affairs as one's own and nothing more. Accordingly, the way of the loyal retainer is to leave nothing undone. Indeed, sacrificing one's life in the name of "Righteousness" falls within the bounds of "seeing another person's affairs as one's own." After all, the Way of the Sages is a way for governing the country, and thus this definition of Loyalty differs from the conventional sense of the word. The key difference is between a superior's entrusting something to an inferior and an inferior's entrusting something to a superior. In current social practice, superiors do not entrust things to inferiors—as a result, retainers have the mentality of day laborers. High officials on the monthly rotation system not worrying about what they leave to their successors represents an example of what Pan Ku called "consuming a salary without lifting a finger."[69] It is evidence, too, of their not seeing their bodies as their own. Seeing oneself as the property of others is the way of concubines and wives.

69. Pan Ku, *Hou-han shu,* Chu-yun ch'uan.

Women are creatures who entrust themselves to others and thus are reluctant to advance their own ideas. They leave matters to their husbands.

Retainers receive orders from their lords and regard their assigned position and rank as their own personal affair. If their lord's order is at odds with their own ideals or makes them uneasy, retainers resign their positions out of a fear of being disloyal. When retainers do not see themselves as their own property, they do not advance their own ideas and are simply at the mercy of their lords. When this happens, the lord is completely alone: he has retainers, but it is as though they did not exist. Retainers are a lord's assistants, not his personal toys. The practice of treating retainers as toys originates in the mistake mentioned earlier—namely, the idea that a retainer's body is not his own property—and this violates the Way of the Sages. From the lord's point of view, the issue is entrusting or not entrusting matters to his retainers. To the retainer, the question is considering or not considering his lord's affairs as his own. A retainer's agreeing with his lord and saying little separates the minds of the high and the low. All of this begins with a misunderstanding of the word "loyalty." This, I believe, is a matter that deserves the most careful consideration.

Reform

19. Your ideas on political matters seem reasonable, but I do not think they get to the heart of the matter. The Way of the Sages has the revering of Heaven and the ancestors as its foundation. As your province was entrusted to you by Heaven and bequeathed to you by your ancestors, it would be absurd for you to regard it as your own possession. It is said that the laws of one's ancestors should not be changed. If you had been born when the province was being developed, no matter what the issue, you could have had your way. Your changing the old laws and creating new ones in this province passed on to you by your ancestors would be an abuse of your freedom. You would not be revering your ancestors, and this would cause quite a little harm. More specifically, it would be like those who are given a province and become lords procuring land and building another mansion, or the recipients of a province left to them by their forebears living in an old house built by someone else. Were the new owners to refurbish this old house, no matter what they did, the original owner's preferences

would not be theirs, and the house could never be sufficiently renovated. If they renovated according to their preferences, removing a
pillar here and taking out a wall there, ceiling joists would begin to
sag and pillars would bend in unexpected places, and those sagging
joists and bending pillars would weaken the house, causing more
problems than existed before the renovations were begun. Those who
do not live in the kind of old house that poor folk like me dwell in
cannot understand this parable.

People like me, who have just turned fifty, have trouble with lumbago, spasms, and congestion. If you took someone with poor circulation to Pien Ch'üeh, even he could not restore that person's state of
health to what it was when that person was twenty. Long-term illnesses cannot be healed, no matter what the cure. Unskilled physicians err in relying on their initial diagnosis and trying to control
everything—as a result, their patients never recover but lose their
energy and find their lives shortened. When one has truly understood
this principle, one realizes that the ancient saying "our ancestors'
methods should not be changed" is right on the mark. Inasmuch as
you are not conversant with the way of order and disorder, prosperity
and decline, and are not familiar with human emotion and social customs and consider only the short-term advantages and disadvantages
of things and whether they bring immediate profit or loss, your revision of the ancient laws of the province would be most unwise.

The people are comfortable with what they are used to. Things that
have been done over and over for some time began to leave their
imprint several generations ago, even before you were born, and thus
even something that is bad is regarded as good. The people of the
world are interdependent, complementary, and one body. And this is
why the affairs to which they have become accustomed over the years
have taken root and spread in all directions. Many have profited by
relying on this. If you were suddenly to change all of this, deficiencies
and distortions would appear here and there, where you least expect
them. This is worth thinking about.

The Duke of Chou's profound reflections are to be found in the
commentaries on the *Book of History*. Knowledge of the Sages keeps
one from making drastic changes, and this is especially true when one
establishes a new province. Although it is said that one institutes
whatever one pleases, what does this mean? The distinctions made
between right and wrong according to principle are not the true right

and wrong. Rather, they all are immediate preferences. In the final analysis, there still are traces of the Neo-Confucian philosophy of principle in your thinking, and so your knowledge and wisdom are shallow and wanting. Here I have presumed on your kindness and presented my own views.

Transmigration

20. You have made several inquiries about transmigration and rebirth. However, I am a practitioner of Confucianism, not Buddhism, and because transmigration and rebirth emerge in Buddhist theories, you would do better to ask a Buddhist. The Sung Confucians use the doctrines of principle and material force to refute transmigration, but this is purely speculative. They have not seen hell with their own eyes, and it is on theoretical grounds that they deny the existence of transmigration. The Buddhists' claims about the existence of hells is speculation as well. Confucians and Buddhists are hardly the only ones who do this. Speculative statements are always a matter of conjecture, and conjecture is never a sure thing. What it comes down to is this: Buddhists believe in Buddha's words and insist on transmigration. I myself do not believe in Buddhism; I believe in the Sages. When something is not mentioned in the Sages' teachings—even if, for example, transmigration really exists—I do not give it much thought. My point is that because the Sages' teachings are sufficient in all ways, I truly believe that nothing is lacking, and it is in this way that my view of things is determined. Having said that, however, I am not suggesting that you adopt my views. I have given you my own views only because you asked about these matters.

Ancestral and Heavenly Spirits

21. The question of the existence or nonexistence of ancestral and heavenly spirits has been the subject of noisy debates in both the past and the present.[70] All these debates have been theoretical, however, and as a theory is just a lot of talk, none is fully credible. The classics of the Sages suggest that ancestral and heavenly spirits do indeed

70. Although *kishin* (C. *kuei-shen*) is usually translated "ghosts and spirits," when Sorai uses this term he is referring to what he called "heavenly spirits" (J. *tenjin*) and "ancestral spirits" (J. *jinki*). See Sorai, *Benmei, NST,* 36:237–238.

exist. The Sung Confucians, with their conceptions of principle, material force, and yin and yang, have had a lot to say about this matter, but their statements might be described as merely their own interpretations and not the august pronouncements of the Sages. Those who follow the Sung Confucians' theories end up concluding that ancestral and heavenly spirits do not exist. Because this conclusion diverges from the Sages' teachings, it is hard to accept. In the Sages' writings is a way of governing ancestral and heavenly spirits, which, if used, finds these spirits benefiting, not harming, the world. Having said this, there is nothing more to say.

The theories of the Buddhists, Taoists, and shamans offer methods for pacifying ancestral and heavenly spirits, but all are detrimental to the way of governing the country. Because they differ from the Sages' writings, these theories should not command the credence of Gentlemen. It is not for mortals to look deeply into the depths of what is unknowable and to speculate on the nature of ancestral and heavenly spirits. Even if one understood ancestral and heavenly spirits, there is no way of pacifying these spirits except with the Sages' teachings, and this is why one should steer clear of this issue.

Laws

22. In reading your letter, I noticed a divergence from the laws of the year before last, and I understand why this was the case. Your losing the trust of the populace is unfortunate. If the general population does not trust their superiors, they will not submit to them. People will continually wonder whether they are being deceived, and this will make them inattentive, suspicious, and fearful. If you encourage the people to be fearful, the laws will stand no chance of being implemented. Because the people are lowly creatures, their rulers will never know whether they are really afraid of their superiors, and simply imagining that they are would be very foolish indeed. Confucius gave us the parable of the yokebar and collarbar: "Master said, I do not see what use a man can be put to, whose word cannot be trusted. How can a wagon be made to go if it has no yokebar or a carriage, if it has no collarbar?"[71] If rulers are not trusted by their people, they cannot govern. Teachers who are not trusted by their students cannot teach. It

71. *Lun-yü*, II:22; Waley, *Analects*, p. 93.

is a psychological constant that when people are with friends, and others as well, if they have doubts they grow apart, and if they trust one another they grow closer. The Way of the Sages is like this.

Heaven's Will

23. As for the matter in question, what you ask is reasonable, but I would guess that you were deeply shocked by what I said. If, up to now, your administration has not been responsive to Heaven's will, then shocked though you may be, you cannot escape its punishment. Nothing is quite as good as revering Heaven, correcting one's errors, and cultivating one's virtue—and there are no methods for worshiping Heaven outside of the Sages' teachings. Even if you do all of these things, Heaven may not change its mind—and if Heaven refuses to change its mind, there is no escaping its mandate. Being shocked will not help. It is said that "a fool never prevails over virtue" and that "a fool rises by means of others."[72] Strange things, it is said, result from a disordered mind.[73] If a great general is anxious, there will be no dispel-

72. The first passage is from the *Shih-chi*, Yen-chi, and the second is from the *Ch'un-ch'iu*, Chuang-kung shih-ssu nien.
73. Sorai may be alluding to "portents such as these are born from disorder," which occurs in a discussion of "strange occurrences" in the "Discussion of Heaven" chapter of the *Hsün-tzu*. The entire passage reads:
  Among all such strange occurrences, the ones really to be feared are human portents. When the plowing is poorly done and the crops suffer; when the weeding is badly done and the harvest fails; when the government is evil and loses the support of the people; when the fields are neglected and the crops are badly tended; when grain must be imported from abroad and sold at a high price, and the people are starving and die by the roadside—these are what I mean by human portents. When government commands are unenlightened, public works are undertaken at the wrong season, and agriculture is not properly attended to, these too are human portents. When the people are called away for *corvee* labor at the wrong season, so that cows and horses are left to breed together and the six domestic animals produce prodigies; when ritual principles are not obeyed, family affairs and outside affairs are not properly separated, and men and women mingle wantonly, so that fathers and sons begin to doubt each other, superior and inferior become estranged, and bands of invaders enter the state—these too are human portents. Portents such as these are born from disorder, and if all three types occur at once, there will be no safety for the state. The reasons for their occurrence may be found very close at hand; the suffering they cause is great indeed. You should not only wonder at them but fear them as well.
See Watson, *Hsün-tzu*, pp. 84–85.

ling the anxiety of his underlings. Indeed, Confucius said: "He who does not understand the will of heaven cannot be regarded as a gentleman."[74] The resolution of those who do not know Heaven's will is uncertain. I have responded frankly to your questions. Respectfully yours.

Orders and Regulations

24. You have been kind enough to show me samples of your orders and regulations. The quality of their substance aside, their language is rather unfelicitous. Although you do not offer detailed explanations, you seem not to realize that orders and regulations should not have to be explained. There is a certain unreasonableness in what you have shown me, which may be why you wonder whether your subjects will be persuaded and why you spelled out things so carefully. Given their unreasonableness, it is best that these orders and regulations not be implemented. If, in contrast, you issue an order or regulation that will benefit your subjects, they should be made to obey it, even if they are not persuaded of its value. Detailed explanation is unnecessary. The point is that because the general population is stupid, rulers should think carefully before they make pronouncements. The people will not realize that an order or regulation is "for their benefit" until much later. It is like getting a child to understand something one part at a time. It is pointless.

It is precisely because the status of rulers and subjects is different that pampering the people always causes so much harm. I am not sure I understand why this has become so common in recent years. That we want our subjects to commend our talent and knowledge and to recognize our virtuous deeds signals a decline in our status as rulers. The saying in the *Analects,* "He who remains unsoured when not recognized is ... a Gentleman," pertains to rulers: those who rule have Heaven as their companion and thus have no interest in being known by their subjects.[75] When rulers ignore their subjects, they have trouble gaining positions and carrying out the way, which is why they insist on being recognized. The ancients never gained the positions they deserved and went unrecognized, despite their having the virtues of rulers, yet they were not bothered by this. In contrast, those who

74. *Lun-yü,* XX:3; Waley, *Analects,* p. 233.
75. *Lun-yü,* I:1.

hold positions today make mistakes on their own, which may be why their subjects ignore their orders.

Remonstrations

25. As for remonstrating rulers, it is best not done. If you do it often, you will be humiliated, because it is usually impossible to enlighten someone verbally. Usually things worth mentioning are already known to the other party. Moreover, people's ideas differ according to whether or not they have realized something on their own. Not surprisingly, those who have not realized something on their own rarely appreciate having it explained to them. Confucius observed that "subtle admonitions" are fine, and the phrase "simply handed in through the window" in the *Book of Changes* suggests that it is best to allow a person to realize something naturally.[76] There are occasions when, if one ignores the matter in question and brings up something else, the person with whom you are speaking will understand. If you bicker with people over the rightness or wrongness of an issue, they will get upset, then truly exercised, and an argument will most certainly ensue. Wanting to win an argument is like wanting to win a military battle, and the anger of the involved parties never subsides. When addressing a ruler, one should not expect to be heard. A ruler's seeking remonstrances, however, is quite another matter, and when one is deeply trusted by the ruler, one's suggestions will be heeded. This is true not only for remonstrations. Generally speaking, it is pointless to explain something to someone who does not trust you.

In our time, remonstrating with rulers and presenting one's views usually means puffing oneself up before strangers. This is the mentality of someone involved in a legal case and is thus like being in the midst of a battle. What happens? The remonstrance spurs the lord on to greater misdeeds; the critic loses his life; his advice is ignored; and he is remembered as a "remonstrating retainer." This being the case, remonstrances are the work not of loyal retainers but of those eager to make a name for themselves. You should understand this. But officeholders who immerse themselves in their work and see it as their own will, on occasion, have something that they must say to their lord. Handle these cases as the occasion requires.

76. *I-ching*, K'an, hexagram number 29; Wilhelm, *I Ching*, p. 117.

Transforming One's Nature

26. You indicated that you are extremely worried about what you regard as your unusually unpleasant disposition. It is true that acknowledging your faults is a good thing, but seeing yourself in this way is not very healthy. One's inborn nature is endowed by Heaven and produced by one's own father and mother. The idea of transforming one's innate nature is an empty Sung Confucian theory, and forcing people to be what they are not is most unreasonable. The inborn nature, no matter what one does to it, resists transformation: a grain of rice is forever a grain of rice; a bean is forever a bean. Simply nourishing one's innate nature and developing it as it was at birth are the essence of education. It is like fertilizing rice or bean plants so they produce as their heavenly natures dictate. The husk is not of any use—and no matter what one does to it, it will never be of any use. Thus a grain of rice is useful to the world as a grain of rice, and a bean is useful as a bean. But a grain of rice will never become a bean; nor will a bean ever become a grain of rice. If, following Sung Confucian theory, one transformed one's innate nature and achieved that "indeterminate and harmonious state," is this not like a grain of rice or a bean wanting to be something else? That could not possibly be of any benefit. And as for a grain of rice becoming a bean and a bean being used as a grain of rice, this sort of thing does not happen in the world. These all are empty theories produced by the quest for sagehood.

The Sages were endowed by Heaven with intelligence and wisdom, and their brilliance matched that of the gods. How can one speak of achieving this by human effort? As no one—from antiquity onward—has succeeded in becoming a sage, the fallaciousness of this Sung Confucian theory should be obvious. Nowhere in the Sages' teachings is one told "to become a sage." If one follows the Sages' teachings, one will instead become a Gentleman. The Sung Confucians accept, and even mimic, the Buddhists' injunction to become a buddha by means of the way of the Buddha. In Sung Confucian theory, sages are those who have completely purified their desires and have become one with heavenly principle, yet those in this state are hardly sages. Conjuring up sages in this way is like painting thunder and ancestral spirits. A young girl who thinks that the unseen phenomena that she imagines and paints truly exist—that thunder is the beating of giant drums and that ancestral spirits wear tiger-skin undergarments—is not far from those who, following Sung Confucian theory, invent conceptions of sages. Subscribing to the Sages' and Sung Confucians' teachings are this different. You should think carefully about this.

27. As I observed in an earlier letter, because you know little about the Way of the Sages, your thinking is not very profound.[77] You think only of remedying what is immediate, what is at the tip of your nose. Human beings are active creatures. Thus governing the country, instructing people, and even cultivating one's own mind and body are not like carving a doll out of a piece of wood. Curing an illness is much the same. Physicians who conclude from their patients' symptoms that they need only to suppress a cough, stop the vomiting, cool a fever, or restore a lost appetite are not very accomplished. Physicians who understand the Way are different, which is why one speaks of the Way of the Sages as the "Method of the Great Way." Governing a country is not simply a matter of attending to good and evil, the correct and incorrect, and dealing with what is visible. By working from points the uninitiated would never think of, one remedies the situation naturally without anyone's being aware of this or knowing that it is happening. One nourishes human talent in the same way. Owing to a distaste for what is known in society as "deceptive methods," there is little or no discussion of the questions of "methods," and when there is, it sounds like the Sung Confucians' theories. If you ignored the various theories of later generations and mastered the Six Classics and the *Analects of Confucius,* you would naturally come to understand what I have been saying.

Filial Piety

28. You asked about the practice of Filial Piety. In the Sages' teachings, Filial Piety, Brotherly Respect, Loyalty, and Trust are called "the virtuous acts of the *Doctrine of the Mean*" and are described as ceremonial forms that everyone, whether noble or mean, should carry

---

77. The "way" for Sorai was always the "Way of the Sages and Early Kings."

out.[78] If the way of the Gentleman were not based on these virtuous acts, it would be like climbing to a high place without a ladder. Shun's appointing Chieh as the minister of education and having him teach the Five Relations to the people has the same import as Confucius' lamenting the absence of the virtue of the Mean among the general population.[79]

"Filial Piety" entails serving one's parents. "Brotherly Respect" entails serving one's elder brother. "Loyalty" entails taking on and doing for others—whether a lord or anyone else—what one would do for oneself. "Trust" requires speaking carefully and not lying or making mistakes in one's dealings with friends and others as well. All these virtuous acts implicate the way of fathers and mothers, elder and younger brothers, rulers and subjects, and friends—which is why when one speaks of the Five Relations, the *Doctrine of the Mean,* or Filial Piety, Brotherly Respect, Loyalty, or Trust, one is referring to the same thing. Filial Piety and Brotherly Respect receive more attention because as long as children are still living with their parents, neither the ruler–subject relationship nor that between friends applies. If Filial Piety is seen as primary, this is because no one is without a father and a mother, although some are without older or younger brothers. Moreover, Filial Piety and Brotherly Respect are easy for children to understand and help them grasp the ways of Loyalty, Trust, and the Five Relations. This is the reason why Filial Piety and Brotherly Respect have priority in the teachings of the Early Kings. Filial Piety, Brotherly Respect, Loyalty, and Trust are called the "virtuous acts of the *Doctrine of the Mean*" because anyone—no matter how stupid, talented, or informed—can perform them. They are given this designation because they are not particularly elevated affairs.

That the way of the Gentleman has these virtuous acts as its foundation is because it is Humanity. Here Humanity refers to the pacifi-

78. I render *koto* (C. *shih*) as "ceremonial form" rather than the more conventional "thing," "object," or "affair" because this rendering is closer to the Chou usage of the word, which Sorai preferred to the Neo-Confucian usage. In Eastern Chou (771–221 B.C.) works such as the *Analects* and *Lao-tzu,* the term *shih* is used to refer to ritual norms and etiquette. See *Lun-yü,* I:14, III:15, X:14, XII:1–2, XIII:3, and *Lao-tzu,* 2, 3, and 31. That Sorai used the word *koto/shih* in this way is clear. First, he spoke repeatedly of "rehearsing the ceremonial forms" (C. *hsi shih,* J. *koto o narau*); second, neither "thing" nor "object" would make much sense here. See Sorai, *Benmei, NST,* 36:249–250, 253; *Chūyōkai, NMSCZ,* 1:3.
79. *Shih-chi,* Wu-ti penchi, shun, and *Lun-yü,* VI:29.

cation of the general population of the provinces and the realm; originally, it was the way of those who ruled. The virtuous acts of the *Doctrine of the Mean*—Filial Piety, Brotherly Respect, Loyalty, and Trust—apply to everyone according to their status and not just to those who rule. Filial Piety is the way of nurturing one's father and mother and making them comfortable. Brotherly Respect is the way of nurturing and putting at ease one's elder and younger brothers. Loyalty is the way of serving one's lord and nurturing and putting him at ease. Trust is the way of putting at ease and nourishing one's friends. This being so, you should see all of these virtuous acts as facets of Humanity.

There is, however, the question of ability. It would be difficult for those without the requisite ability to accept Humanity as their responsibility. You should realize that regardless of how much or how little ability people have, their fulfilling the spirit of Humanity constitutes Filial Piety, Brotherly Respect, Loyalty, Trust, and the "virtuous acts of the *Doctrine of the Mean*." Accordingly, if one makes Filial Piety, Brotherly Respect, Loyalty, and Trust the foundation and starts out from this point, one's actions will correspond completely to the Humanity of the Gentleman. If, however, one does not make Filial Piety, Brotherly Respect, Loyalty, and Trust the foundation and seeks only to carry out the policies that will bring order to the provinces and realm, then one will make the mistake of rushing to heterodox methods of governing. Tzu Ssu and others wrote about what they did to prevent this from happening.[80] Although the particular term in the Sages' teachings will differ according to the student's ability, there is only one way and no other. You should think very carefully about this.

Literature

29. You regard the study of poetry and prose as a useless affair. This is understandable, given that you have been listening for years to the Sung Confucians' talk about "poetry and prose, memorization and recitation." You should know, first of all, that the Five Classics include what is known as the *Book of Odes*. The *Odes* is analogous

80. Tzu Ssu was Confucius' grandson and the author of the *Doctrine of the Mean*.

to our *waka* and does not discuss the principles of self-cultivation or the way to govern the provinces and realm.[81] The *Odes* contains the ancients' utterances of pain and pleasure, words that accord well with universal human emotions, words of the highest refinement, words that allow one to know the customs of a particular country at a specific time. The Sages collected these words and taught them to the people. Although studying the *Book of Odes* will not help one master principles, the poetry of the *Odes* uses language with such consummate skill, presents the range of human emotion so well, and is so impressive that one's feelings will naturally deepen and one's powers of ratiocination will be refined. Moreover, the *Odes* enables one to understand the customs of a society or a province, which are hard to grasp theoretically. It brings one's own feelings into line with universal emotions. It allows those of high status to know the affairs of the lowly, men to fathom the workings of women's minds, and the intelligent to understand the stupid. The language of the *Odes* is highly refined and has the power to make people understand things that are left unsaid. It has many other benefits as well: it is useful in teaching and when offering subtle admonitions. That there is something called gentlemanly manners and customs, which is distinct from theory, would be hard to grasp without knowledge of the *Odes*. All the poetry and prose of later generations have the *Odes* as their locus classicus, and because our age is close to that of the *Odes,* many passages are easy to understand.[82] This is why those who study the *Odes* with this in mind will be amply rewarded.

This is especially true when engaging in scholarship in our country. That is, because the Sages were Chinese and the classical texts are written in Chinese, the Way of the Sages is difficult to grasp without a knowledge of Chinese characters. As for acquiring this knowledge, if

81. The *waka* is a classical form of Japanese poetry that first appeared in the seventh century and survives into the present. Consisting of thirty-one syllables organized in lines of 5–7–5–7–7, *waka* were typically lyrical and an important vehicle for personal expression. From the outset, it was distinguished from verse written in Chinese, or *kanshi.*

82. Sorai had long believed that the "feelings and customs" (J. *ninjō setai*) of his age were close to those of ancient China. "Although people are forever talking about how the ancients and moderns differ from one another," he once wrote, "I discovered when I read the works of the Three Dynasties that their authors' *feelings and customs* were the same as ours" (my italics). See Sorai, *Daigen jūsoku, MOSZ,* 2:6.

one is unable to duplicate the consciousness of the ancients when they wrote those texts, one's knowledge will never be complete. Thus if one does not actually compose poetry and prose in Chinese, there will be much that remains beyond one's understanding. Those who have studied only the classics will not have mastered Chinese, and their understanding will be imperfect and artificial. This is why poetry and prose are so important to Japanese scholars. Although *waka* and such things are reminiscent of the *Odes*, their feminine manner is evidence that ours is a country without sages. Although what I have just said does not apply to you, if you understand what is meant by "elegance," you will never lose your gentlemanly disposition, which will be valuable to you as a ruler. The teachings of the philosophy of principle have been seeping into the contemporary consciousness for some time, and so people do not understand the usefulness of the useless. Frequently, they are anxious about most things and turn their backs on the Way of the Sages. You should be careful about this.

Divination

30. Although the phenomenon called "divination" occurs in the Sages' writings, you admit that you find it hard to accept.[83] This is typical of those who embrace the philosophy of principle. You are skeptical because you have accepted these narrow views. It is because of the idea that theory explains everything that you do not accept divination.

Scapulimancy and divination by milfoil stalks appear to be "ways of fortune telling," by which I mean ways of dispelling doubts. The divination that women and children prefer nowadays is simply a means of knowing whether the future holds good or bad fortune, whether it is lucky or not. Yet knowing today that you will die tomorrow is of no value. Ancient scapulimancy and milfoil divination were not at all like this. If, for example, there were a fork in the road and uncertainty about whether one should go to the left or to the right and if the principle governing the situation were unclear and deliberation did not help, one would consult ancestral and heavenly spirits by using scapulimancy and milfoil divination. When there was nothing of concern, there were no prognostications about whether the year would bring good or bad fortune. This is "fortune telling."

83. For a full discussion of divination, see Sorai, *Benmei, NST,* 36:239.

In the *Book of Changes,* there is the phrase "starting things and completing affairs."[84] "Starting things" refers to beginning something. Everything that has existed up to now and what the people are used to doing is not a concern, and thus nothing else is needed. As for initiating something that has not been done before, it is precisely because the general population is not used to doing it that there is no one to coordinate their efforts. No matter what it is, if one works hard, one will complete the task; if one does not work hard, one will not—this is a logical constant of principle. Using scapulimancy and milfoil divination to clarify the benefits and profits that will result is a way of unifying the minds of the people and urging them on; in the end the task will be completed. This is what is meant by "disclosing things and completing affairs."

Generally speaking, there are limits to human knowledge and power in regard to the affairs of the world. Because heaven and earth, like human beings, are active phenomena, the interaction of human beings with heaven and earth and with one another can change endlessly, and there is no predicting what will happen. When fools discover that one or two things went as they thought they would, they believe they were able to do this by means of their own intellectual power. This is not the case at all, however. They accomplished what they did with the help of heaven and earth, ancestral and heavenly spirits. In situations beyond human knowledge and power, the Gentleman, knowing Heaven's will, remains calm and works at what he is to carry out and, as a result, naturally gains the help of heaven and earth and ancestral and heavenly spirits. Fools, in contrast, discover little by means of their own knowledge, and the result is doubt, distraction, and a diminishing will to work. Accordingly, their projects crumble and are never realized.

Consider, for example, the captain of a ship. When he boards a vessel, his shipboard activities have their own principles, and one finds him using all of his knowledge of such things. Yet once he is on the open sea and at the mercy of the wind and the waves, he quickly exhausts his knowledge and finds that he is in the hands of Buddha and the spirits. Yet simply relying on the power of Buddha and spirits and throwing away the oars and rudder and prostrating oneself on

84. *I-ching,* Hsi-tz'u ch'uan; Wilhelm, *I Ching,* p. 316. I have altered Wilhelm's translation slightly.

the floor of the boat is not the way to stay alive. Besides relying on the power of Buddha and the spirits, one must do what has to be done and in this way transcend the difficulties of ten deaths and one life and thus stay alive.

Then again, when one ventures out onto a battlefield, no matter how famous a general he might be, things are never as clear as they are to a skilled *go* player. In *go,* there is the board: an inert thing marked off with crossing lines and 361 points. The stones that one plays are inert as well. One calmly ponders each move, and skilled players easily anticipate future moves. But the way of war is not executed on a *go* board. Instead one is handling—as a mass—creatures who are themselves active and rushing about. This is why from ancient times military tactics have included divining by means of cloud formations, the wind, scapulas, and milfoil stalks and using magic to vanquish the enemy. All are ways of uniting the minds of the ignorant masses and getting them to work at a task. In this respect the past and the present are as one.

The disadvantage of the philosophy of principle is that all its practitioners are small-minded and, like crabs digging holes, see everything solely in terms of themselves. This may be why at some point they forgot that the Way of the Sages is a way of governing the provinces and the realm. Even their discussions of the task of governing the provinces and pacifying the realm become a matter of the mind that knows the abstract principles of government—with no attention paid to implementing what one knows. Worse yet, they believe that even the Mandate of Heaven, which is beyond the ken and power of humans, can be reached with principle. Owing to your having studied the Sung Confucians' philosophy of principle, you do not understand the idea of using the Sages' methods of divination by scapulimancy and milfoil stalks. When your scholarly attainments grow and as you become a person of broad capacity, your doubts will be dispelled. At the outset, you should understand that the fundamentals are as I have presented them.

Way of the Warrior

31. You asked whether what is commonly called the "way of the warrior" accords with the way of the Gentleman as described in ancient texts and the way of governing people. No matter what the

philosophy, if you start discussing its underlying principles, they always will deal with ways of governing the provinces and the realm. The naturalism of Lao-tzu and Chuang-tzu and the legalism of Shen Pu-hai and Han Fei-tzu were, from the outset, ways of governing the country.[85] You also should consider Hsü Hsing's agricultural practices, Pien Ch'üeh's medical techniques, Kuo T'uo-t'uo's aboriculture, and the theories of Yang Tsung-yüan's head carpenter.[86] What is known today as the way of war is, in most cases, the principles of the famous generals of the Warring States period passed on by military theorists and others. Because the way of the warrior was originally a way for governing provinces and commanding knights and foot soldiers, it is not without its good points. Compared with the Way of the Sages, what can one say makes it superior?

When discussing the Way, it is best to begin with people. Because the worth or worthlessness, strengths and weaknesses, of figures like Minamoto Yoritomo, Ashikaga Takauji, and Kusunoki Masashige in the distant past and Takeda Shingen and Uesugi Kenshin in recent times are well known, the principles that comprise the Way are, ultimately, knowable.[87] As for those who succeeded T'ai Kung-wang, who is represented in the ancient texts—and here I include Sun-tzu, Wu-tzu, Han Hsin, Chu-ke Kung-ming, and Li Ching—they are

85. Shen Pu-hai (d. 337 B.C.) was chancellor of the state of Han; Han Fei-tzu (d. 233 B.C.) was a prince in the same state. Both are regarded as the founders, together with Shang Yang (d. 338 B.C.) and Li Ssu (d. 208 B.C.), of a philosophical movement known as Legalism. The *Han Fei-tzu* is the most famous Legalist classic.

86. As noted earlier, Pien Ch'üeh was a famous Warring States physician and the author of *The Classic of Difficult Issues (Nan-ching)*. Hsü Hsing appeared at the court of Duke Wen of T'eng and proposed that rulers farm together with their subjects. Kuo T'uo-t'uo was a famous hunchbacked gardener. And the reference to Yang Tsung-yüan's carpenter is mysterious; Yang, of course, was a leading T'ang litterateur.

87. Minamoto Yoritomo (1147–1199) was the founder of the first military government, the Kamakura *bakufu*. Ashikaga Takauji (1305–1358) fought on the side of imperial forces in the event known as the Kemmu Restoration (1334) but betrayed his former allies at a critical moment and installed himself as the head of a new military government, the Ashikaga *bakufu*. He is conventionally seen as the epitome of betrayal and duplicity. Kusunoki Masashige (d. 1336) was a famous warrior general who died fighting for the imperial cause and resisting Takauji to the end. Takeda Shingen and Uesugi Kenshin (1530–1578) were Warring States lords who distinguished themselves in the battles that raged in the mid-sixteenth century.

revered as teachers by our various schools of military science.[88] Yet none of these personages created anything called the "way of war."

In regard to the origins of the way of war, we have the expression "letters and the martial arts: two ways." It has been customary since the medieval period, when the nobility and warriors were separated, to call the arts transmitted by the nobility the "way of letters" and those passed on by the warriors the "way of war."[89] Poetry and song as well as archery and horsemanship are arts, but an ignorant person once referred to them as the way, and this is how one speaks of them now. Owing to the hereditary nature of warrior offices, specific customs have naturally come into being. Valuing courage, accepting death, knowing shame, honoring sincerity, not committing thoughtless and depraved acts—these established practices have existed from the time of the Minamoto and the Taira.[90] After that, the world was a congeries of warring states, and everyone used military laws and rules to govern the provinces. Later, even after the Tokugawa unified the realm, they were like blind men who did not know enough to learn from the past and to return to literary virtues. Until the present age of great peace, civil officers continued to discharge military functions and provincial governments still used military laws and orders. Accordingly, using force to quash the enemy and always preferring the easy and straightforward way of doing things was established as the warrior form of government. The ignorant

88. Sorai introduces the most famous Chinese military men and thinkers: Sun Tzu (fourth century B.C.), author of the classic treatise on war, the *Sun Tzu*; Wu Tzu (sixth century B.C.), a general serving the state of Wei and the author of the *Wu Tzu*; Han Hsin (d. 196 B.C.), a Han general famous for his use of kites in siege warfare; Chu-ke Kung-ming (181–234), inventor of a new type of crossbow and the wheelbarrow; and Li Ching (571–644), a superb military strategist and tactician who oversaw the T'ang dynasty's campaigns against troublesome Turko-Mongol tribes.

89. The distinction between the civil and military arts is originally Chinese, appearing in the *Book of Odes* and the *Han Fei-tzu*. The phrase "letters and the martial arts are two paths, and abandoning any one is impossible" occurs in a T'ang work, *Imperial Norms* (Ti-fan) See *Ti-fan,* Chung-wen.

90. The Minamoto and Taira were provincial warrior families who emerged, along with many others, in the tenth century. They served the civil government in Kyoto, filling the post of police commissioner and providing men for the palace guards, even as they fought among themselves. They were the strongest of these families and had been fighting for over a century when the Minamoto, under Yoritomo and Yoshitsune (1159–1189), prevailed in 1185 and founded the first military government.

believe that this is the way of the warrior transmitted from ancient times in our country.

Military theorists have studied bits and pieces of Confucian texts; combined things like the virtues of Creativity, Sublimity, Firmness, and Strength; read them into the accounts of famous Warring States generals; and claim that the way of the warrior is the way of the gods.[91] Given their glorification of the way of the warrior, it sounds as though this is as it should be, but in fact all of this dates from the Warring States period and did not exist until the age of the Minamoto and Taira. Because order has prevailed in the world for some time and customs have changed, warrior customs dating from the time of the Minamoto and the Taira have deteriorated, and the customs of the Warring States era are now popular.

After all, the word "military" is glossed "prevailing over rebellion," and "quelling disorder and rebellion" is now used to define the word "military." The original sense of the word "military" comes from pacifying the population with a Humane mind, which includes quelling rebellions and disorder and quieting the domains, but this is one side of the Way of the Sages. In times of order, one uses the literary arts; in times of disorder, the martial arts. There is just one Way, however, and it could hardly be the case that the Way could contain both a "way of letters" and a "way of war."

People are born with physical natures that have specific dispositions, which is why there are literary virtues and martial virtues. Even within bureaucratic posts, there are a myriad administrative tasks, and thus are there civil and military officials. Because positions like that of platoon captain and commander are military offices, those with military virtues are appropriate choices. With the positions of house elder and magistrate, which are civil offices, someone lacking literary virtues would not be suitable. Ordinary warriors are simply higher-rank foot soldiers organized by unit and specialty, and because they serve in peacetime as palace guards, they are hardly of the same ilk as the knights and gentlemen mentioned in the ancient texts. For the lords of provinces and commanderies, house elders, magistrates,

91. Following Richard Wilhelm, I translate *kan, yüan, kang,* and *ch'ien* as "creativity," "sublimity," "firmness," and "strength." These are archaic terms that first appear in divinatory formulas on oracle bones dating from the Shang dynasty (1751–1111 B.C.) and in the oldest strata of the *Book of Changes.*

and the like to see themselves as warriors is a gross misconception. And as for those ordinary warriors who, possessing a modicum of learning, fancy themselves as knights or gentlemen, comport themselves like the ladies of the Great Interior, stop practicing battlefield tactics, and rehearse only dueling techniques—they are deluding themselves.[92]

Inasmuch as the methods of governing a province presented in the Way of the Sages usually entail following the customs of that province, one should maintain the customs that date from the time of the Minamoto and Taira and eliminate unsalutary practices from the Warring States period. Rulers should know that "the root of the way of the warrior is Humanity"; they should be concerned exclusively with the literary virtues; they should force all warriors to return to the land; they should instill the virtues of Filial Piety, Brotherly Respect, Loyalty, and Trust; and they should maintain the customs of Propriety, Righteousness, Purity, and Shame. From time to time they should require the periodic practice of the military arts, encourage bravery in public matches, and insist on cowardice in private fights.[93] All of this should be done under the ruler's guidance. The problem is that the philosophy of principle has spread throughout society, adding a theoretical dimension to the customs surviving from the Warring States period. This is like using firewood to put out a fire.

Teaching the Untalented

32. You asked how one might instruct those who lack the ability to govern a province or administer political affairs and who should spend all their lives working under others. You presented your view that within the teachings of Zen, Taoism, Chu Hsi, and Wang Yangming are methods of spiritual cultivation that reduce one's anxieties, fears, and confusion about various matters. And you asked, too,

92. The "ladies of the Great Interior" oversaw the life of the shogun's harem, maintaining its etiquette and rituals and supervising the scores of women who served there. They were usually from noble houses.

93. Private combat between warriors had been discouraged from the fourteenth century, and this policy prevailed in Sorai's time as well. Although both parties were usually punished, the attacker was treated more severely. Even so, vendettas were allowed if those intent on avenging a relative or superior had applied for and received official approval from their lord or the appropriate Tokugawa official.

whether other profitable methods exist for governing the minds and bodies of people of limited ability. I understand what you are asking.

In the teachings of the Early Kings, Filial Piety, Brotherly Respect, Loyalty, and Trust are advanced as the virtuous deeds of the *Doctrine of the Mean* that the general population is to perform.[94] As for the way of the Gentleman, which rulers study, it has as its foundation Filial Piety, Brotherly Respect, Loyalty, and Trust and as a supplement the study of the great way of the Gentleman. About other, immediate matters, this stupid old man has no other ideas. When it comes to realizing the ease and pleasure of a mind whose anxieties, fears, and confusion have been quieted, there is nothing in the Way of the Early Kings save being content with the Mandate of Heaven. You must understand that there is nothing else in the Way of the Early Kings but this. There is no mysterious way.

No matter what the issue, those with limited ability see things in terms of themselves and within their own narrow frame of reference. This is why they prefer familiar methods and reduce things to a single dimension. The result: the lesser ways we discussed earlier—the teachings of Zen, Taoism, Chu Hsi, and Wang Yang-ming—which have appeared in the world and command a following. All are the work of those with limited ability. Similar phenomena existed in the age of the Early Kings, and even the Sages were unable to suppress views of this sort. Besides, as each of these philosophies had a certain value, the Sages would never have allowed their suppression. Indeed, using the sorts of lesser ways described above in governing the provinces and realm causes lots of problems, but if one's underlings, who usually do as they please, neither slack off in their posts and family affairs nor ignore Filial Piety, Brotherly Respect, Loyalty, and Trust, this will not be so terrible.

Mastering particular arts gives one additional skills and these become other facets of those who govern provinces. So things like the tea ceremony, flower arranging, *go*, chess, and football may not be intrinsically valuable, but as the *Analects* puts it, "To do these things would surely be better than doing nothing at all."[95] Generally speak-

94. *Chung-yung*, XIX, XX. Here I follow the *Nihon koten bungaku taikei* edition in reading *sensei* as *sennō*. See *NKBT*, 94:209.
95. *Lun-yü*, II:22; Waley, *Analects*, p. 216. I have altered Waley's translation slightly.

ing, people cannot bear to be idle. They do untoward things when their minds lack a focus, and hence those of limited ability are encouraged to be filial, respectful to their brothers, loyal, and trusting and to be allowed to do as they please with all other matters. It would not do any good for you to decide unilaterally just how you want to quiet the minds of those with limited ability. It would look as though you were inclined to use your own favorite methods for any and every matter. Doing this as one governs provinces and oversees their populations is, in my view, quite preposterous.

School Styles

33. You inquired about styles of learning, but this is a hard issue to discuss thoroughly by letter.[96] This is why I have always refused to accept entrance gifts sent from afar.[97] For some years now I have been the recipient of your considerable attention and have done as you wished. Your letter perplexes me.

In the first place, communicating over great distances is obviously difficult. This is why all of Confucius' disciples went to study with him at some point. When one enters a school, one encounters what might be called the "school style," and after being steeped in that school style through various means, one understands quite a lot. The ancient saying "making teachers of one's friends" suggests that it is less a teacher's instructions than the encouragement of friends that broadens one's knowledge and advances one's studies.[98] One cannot say, for example, that the lessons given at present to lords and others of high rank go very well: they employ good teachers and study with them, but because of their rank and wealth, they have no friends, and it seems clear that no matter what they study, they will never master it. Having academic friends and being steeped in a school style is the first issue. Thus, your being so far away obviously impedes our communication.

96. Hiraishi Naoaki, in a personal communication, says that this letter marks the official entry of Mizuno and Hikita into Sorai's school.

97. When one went to study with a teacher or at a private academy, it was customary to offer an "entrance gift." The practice originated in China and was well established in Japan by this time. See Rubinger, *Private Academies of Tokugawa Japan,* pp. 70–71.

98. Sorai is alluding to *Lun-yü,* I:1, IX:24, and XVI:4.

Given your abiding interest, however, I should like to suggest something that might serve as a substitute for teachers and friends.
Although not a perfect substitute, if you use it, your interest will be
rewarded. That substitute for teachers and friends is books. Avoiding
friends who will not help and approaching those who will is the way
to make friends. Thus your eyes should not fall on books that will not
help; you should immerse yourself in books that will. There is no
other substitute for teachers and friends.

If one thinks about the points you raised, it is clear that up to now
you have studied Sung learning exclusively. On the issue of styles of
learning, you should know that a new current emerged in the Sung
dynasty, one that diverged completely from the teachings and methods
of the ancient Sages. Because of this, when one falls into the pit of the
Sung dynasty, one's learning cannot advance. The following should be
seen as "unprofitable friends": Chu Hsi's new commentaries on the
Four Books and Five Classics, *The Complete Works of the Four
Books and Five Classics;* the "classified conversations" of the Sung
Confucians; the poetry and prose of Su Tung-p'o and Huang Shan-ku;
for "poetry in three forms," Chou Pi's *Collection of Poems in Three
Forms* and Fang Hui's *Critical Remarks by Fang Hui;* and for histo-
ries, Chu Hsi's "writing rules" and "clarifications" in *Outline and
Digest of the Great Mirror.*[99] The following should be regarded as
"profitable friends": the best commentaries are those of the ancients,
those of Han and T'ang; the best histories are the *Tso Commentary,
Conversations from the States, Records of the Historian,* and *History
of the Former Han;* the best literary styles are found in *The Songs of*

---

99. Su Tung-p'o (1036–1101) has long been regarded as one of China's greatest
and most versatile writers. A master of several different poetic forms, an esteemed
prose writer, and famous painter and calligrapher, he was admired for his humor,
spontaneity, and sheer brilliance. Huang T'ing-chien (1045–1105) had a distinguished, if difficult, career as a scholar official but is best known as a poet and calligrapher. He promoted a method of poetic composition that he called "changing
the bone" (C. *huan-ku*), which entailed using the imagery and diction of classical
verse and imbuing them with new meanings. *A Collection of Poems in Three
Forms (San-t'i shih-chi),* compiled by Chou Pi in 1250, is one of several "poetry-
writing manuals," as Yoshikawa Kōjirō called them, written for townsmen poets
at the end of the Sung dynasty. *Critical Remarks by Fang Hui (Ying-k'ui lü-sui)* is
a collection of regulated verse from the T'ang and Sung dynasties compiled by a
Sung scholar named Fang Hui (1227–1307). "Writing rules" and "clarifications"
are English translations of Chu Hsi's terms *"shu-fa"* (J. *shohō*) and *"fa-ming"*
(J. *hatsumei*).

the South, Selections of Refined Literature, and the works of Han Yü and Liu Tsung-yüan.[100] As for pre-Han books, even works like the *Lao-tzu, Chuang-tzu,* and *Lieh-tzu* are informative, although the commentaries of Lin Hsi-yi are bad.[101] The best poetry may be found in the *T'ang Poetry Selections* and *Varieties of T'ang Poetry.*[102] The poems of Li Kung-t'ung, Ho Ta-fu, Li Yü-lin, and Wang Yüan-mei are fine, but you will not be able to find them.[103] Before you try to obtain this poetry, you should look at the books mentioned earlier.

Sung Confucians

What I have to say in this letter, because it goes against everything you have thought up to now, should absolutely surprise you, and for this reason I shall be quite specific.

The original ancestors of my Way were Yao and Shun, and Yao and Shun were human rulers. Accordingly, the Way of the Sages is exclusively a way of governing the provinces and realm. The Way is neither the "principle of affairs and things and what should be" nor the "way of heaven, earth, and nature."[104] It is simply the Way that the Sages established. It is a means of governing the provinces and the realm.

---

100. *The Songs of the South (Ch'u-tz'u),* compiled by Wang I in the second century A.D., contains the poems of Ch'u Yüan and others writing in the state of Ch'u late in the Spring and Autumn period (722–481 B.C.). *Selections of Refined Literature (Wen hsüan)* is the oldest surviving collection of Chinese poetry and prose arranged by genre. Although conventionally attributed to Hsiao T'ung (501–531), a prince of the ruling house of the state of Liang, *Selections* is now thought to be the work of Hsiao and a number of collaborators.

101. Lin Hsi-yi was a well-known Sung scholar, calligrapher, and poet whose editions of the *Lao-tzu, Chuang-tzu,* and *Lieh-tzu* circulated widely in Japan.

102. A collection of T'ang poetry attributed to Li P'an-lung (1514–1570), *T'ang Poetry Selections (T'ang Shih-hsüan),* was reprinted in Japan in 1724 and widely read.

103. Li Meng-yang (1472–1529), better known as Li Kung-t'ung, was a member of the Seven Early Masters, a group of poets who favored High T'ang (713–756) poetry and Ch'in–Han (221 B.C.–A.D. 220) prose. Ho Ching-ming (1483–1521), also known as Ho Ta-fu, was one of the Seven Early Masters and shared Li Meng-yang's literary ideals. Li Yu-lin and Wang Yüan-mei (1528–1593), who was also known as Wang Shih-chen, were leading lights in the group known as the Seven Later Masters, and, like Li Meng-yang and Ho Ching-ming, they championed Ch'in–Han prose and High T'ang poetry.

104. These are Neo-Confucian terms, and Sorai is suggesting that they reveal an inability to distinguish the natural and the normative orders.

The Sages' teachings consist solely of ritual and music, which are elegant and refined entities and are nothing like the Neo-Confucians' notion of spiritual cultivation and their penchant for theorizing. With the appearance of the Sung Confucians, people have forsaken actual practice and turned to theory;[105] they have given up elegance and refinement for boorishness and vulgarity. Having forgotten the Way of the Son of Heaven, they are preoccupied with discussions of reason, and making people understand these discussions is their first concern. Because of all this, a battle is raging over what is and what is not reasonable, what is heterodox and what is orthodox. Given the predictability of these arguments, no matter what one learns, one's knowledge and perception are not broadened and there is no progress; one simply becomes one-sided and rigid.

This split reflects pedagogical differences. When the teachings of the Confucian school are compared with those of the Sung Confucians, it is like heaven and earth, clouds and mud. Stylistically, the Sung Confucians' prose is simply *kanamono* written with Chinese characters: it is boorish, shallow, and narrow.[106] Self-immersion in texts such as these keeps one from understanding pre-Han texts of the Three Dynasties. Because you have been unable to grasp this distinction for some time and although what I have said seems not to have penetrated, you are deeply interested in these issues, and thus did I proceed.

Self-Study

Characters comprise the language of the Chinese. In the Japanese language the very nature of words has changed, as has been the case in

---

105. Sorai was critical of what he regarded as the excessive intellectualism of Neo-Confucian conceptions of self-cultivation. He believed that self-cultivation entailed studying and rehearsing the language and ritual etiquette of classical China and, moreover, that it was the actual practice of these archaic Chinese literary and ceremonial forms—what he called "performance" (J. *waza*) or "practice" (J. *okonai*)—that mattered the most. Sorai regarded all other forms of self-cultivation as species of "theory" (J. *rikutsu*).

106. *Kanamono*, literally, "things in the *kana* syllabary," may refer to prose works written in Japanese or a mixture of Japanese and Chinese that appear early in the seventeenth century. Included under this rubric are contemporary fiction, guidebooks, courtesan rankings, and even translations. The audience for these books was decidedly popular and initially, included, warriors and then, later, townsfolk.

China as well. The Sung Confucians' commentaries have lost the ancient language, therefore, but it can be recovered if one makes inferences from ancient texts. The commentaries of later generations differ from the classics on many points. Thus even texts like the *Lao-tzu, Chuang-tzu,* and *Lieh-tzu* are valuable. The Six Classics are the Way, however, and thus if one has mastered the ancient vocabulary but not the Way, one's mastery will not really be complete. This is the reason that those just beginning their studies start with things like the *Tso Commentary, Records of the Historian,* and the *History of the Former Han,* which are easy to read and have many benefits.

If friends living in the same area gather to read texts and do other things together, sometimes east will be mentioned and west will be understood. In far-flung places where one lacks the benefit of friends, scholarship cannot be undertaken very easily. For self-study, nothing equals reading unpunctuated texts. If one can handle a punctuated text, one can handle an unpunctuated text. It is only the eye's being used to the unfortunate practice of reading punctuated texts that keeps one from reading unpunctuated texts. But with hard work, these habits can be changed.

When texts have sections that one does not understand, one gets bored. But if one simply skips over these sections and reads on, one will understand everything later. As for practicing poetry and prose, it is good simply to imitate other poems. If you do this, you will be changed, in time, naturally.[107]

There is nothing more to be said. If there are things that you do not understand, do indicate what they are. The learning that knights acquire enables them to assist the rulers of provinces, to govern their

---

107. Sorai's use of the verb *utsuru*—literally, "to move" but rendered here as "to change"—is significant. Although he used several verbs to describe the process of self-cultivation—*utsuru, kassuru* ("to transform"), *yashinau* ("to nourish"), *narau* ("to get used to"), *oshieru* ("to teach"), and *chōzuru* ("to grow")—he consistently contrasted *utsuru* and *kassuru*. He used the former to refer to the changes that people brought about in themselves through self-cultivation—as in this passage: "It is good simply to imitate other poems. If you do this, in time you will be *changed* naturally" (my italics). The latter, in contrast, referred to changes imposed by others—as, for example, when a government molded its subjects' thought and behavior. Not surprisingly, Sorai usually used *utsuru* when discussing "gentlemen" and *kassuru* when discussing the general population. His usage of *kassuru* has obvious classical sources, chiefly the *Book of Changes* and *Hsün-tzu.*

own households and provinces, and to realize the talent necessary for civil, military, and political affairs. This is the heart of the matter.

Analects of Confucius

You will understand the saying in the *Analects* that "the succession music of King Wu . . . was not perfect Goodness" if you look at the *Book of Music.*[108] Although Confucius mentioned the succession music of Shao and Wu but did not speak of Shun and Wu together, the superiority or inferiority of Yao, Shun, T'ang, and Wu is not discussed. Later generations of Confucians have babbled on and on about the Sages. This is not very valuable and is extremely damaging.

The passage in the *Analects* that reads "Though people may not have shown all that is in them, they are certain to do so when mourning for a father or mother" is saying that those who, when they lose a parent, express their feelings with no regard for ritual are simply showing their grief over the loss.[109] The *Analects* has many passages on ritual.[110] Latter-day Confucians have failed to realize that the Sages' teachings consist exclusively of ritual and music, which is why their interpretations are incorrect.

The passage in the *Analects* that reads "When proper respect towards the dead is shown at the end and continued after they are far away" explains what the Early Kings had in mind when they created ritual.[111] This is not language that is to be used today.

All the compositions you sent me are examples of Sung learning, and so there is no point in my correcting them.

Jottings from a Miscanthus Patch

Jottings from a Miscanthus Patch is a work that I wrote when I was still immature, and so you should not use it.[112] As for the writings of

---

108. *Lun-yü*, III:25. The entire passage reads: "The Master spoke of the succession music of Emperor Shun as being perfect beauty and at the same time perfect goodness, but of that of King Wu as being perfect beauty, but not perfect goodness." See Waley, *Analects*, p. 101; I have altered Waley's translation.

109. *Lun-yü*, XIX:17; Waley, *Analects*, p. 227. I have altered Waley's translation slightly.

110. Sorai is referring to the second half of the *Lun-yü*, chaps. 11–20.

111. *Lun-yü*, I:9; Waley, *Analects*, p. 85. The editors of *Nihon no meicho* suggest that Sorai is thinking of Itō Jinsai here. See *Nihon no meicho*, 16:343.

112. Sorai wrote the pieces collected in *Jottings from a Miscanthus Patch (Ken'en*

Itō Jinsai and Yamazaki Ansai, you absolutely must not read them.[113] It is essential that you ignore what is secondary and study the fundamentals.

The Importance of Studying Literary Style

34. There are points I omitted earlier that I would like to bring up now. Generally speaking, the way of learning involves nothing more than literary style. The way of the ancients is found in texts, and what are texts but literary style? If one has mastered literary style and reads texts on their own terms without adding one's own ideas, the ancients' intentions will be clear. One cannot grasp the Way of the Sages except by following their pedagogy, which survives in texts, and thus everything comes down to literary style.

That literary style and the meaning of words change from age to age and evolve is important. Latter-day Confucians have established their own preferences and regard morality as a noble concern and literary style as a mean pursuit. Their denigration of literary style accounts for their ignorance of the things I mentioned earlier. Accordingly, they fail to understand the pedagogy of the ancient Sages. They use their own personal knowledge to grasp the Way of the Sages and end up creating their own version of the Sages' pedagogy. This group of unlearned scholars have increasingly narrow views, and they believe more deeply in insignificant teachers like the Ch'eng brothers, Chu Hsi, Wang Yang-ming, and, in our country, Yamazaki Ansai and Itō Jinsai, than they do in Confucius. This is

---

zuihitsu) between 1691 and 1712, and they were published in 1/1714. Its strongly worded criticisms of Itō Jinsai created quite a stir, and after its publication, a contemporary source reports, "Sorai was suddenly famous." He later regretted its publication, characterizing it as juvenilia. See his letters to Honda Tadamune, Shimamura Kenshuku, Takeda Shun'an, Asaka Tanpaku, and Hori Keizan, *NST,* 36:516, 517, 527, 528, 538.

113. Yamazaki Ansai (1618–1682) was a leading Neo-Confucian scholar in Kyoto and the founder of the Kimon school. A strict teacher who inspired fear in his students, Ansai claimed to follow the original teachings of Chu Hsi, and his students read nothing else. For a time Ansai advised Hoshina Masayuki (1611–1672), who, with others, served as virtual regents during the minority of the fourth shogun, Tokugawa Ietsuna (1641–1680), and in this capacity influenced government policy.

like the Buddhists' not accepting Buddha's theories but believing in Hōnen and Nichiren.[114]

The Sages' teachings have no past or present, nor does the Way. If one used the Way of the Sages, even the provinces and the realm as they exist today would be ordered; there is nothing else like this. With the Sages' teachings, our contemporaries would realize their talent and virtue; once again, there is no other method that can do this. If they did not run through both the past and present, one would not be discussing the Way and the teachings of the ancient Sages. Both the Sages' Way and their teachings apply to all the people of the realm, among whom the inferior and stupid outnumber the worthy and wise—and this is as true now as it was in the past. Clearly this is why one would never expect the Way and teachings of the ancient Sages to be as difficult as the later Confucians' notion of "principle." Principle is so difficult that those who are stupid cannot fathom it. This is why the Sages' Way and teachings are presented as specific forms of practice. If these are performed, even if their underlying principle is not understood, popular customs will be modified naturally, people's views will be corrected, and order will prevail in the provinces and realm. With these changes in prevailing customs, individuals will broaden their perspectives and realize their talent and virtue. Such is the mysterious effect of the Way of the Sages and their pedagogy.

It is for this reason that contemporary scholarship is trivial and boring and stops at a mastery of literary style. If one understands literary style and has a mastery of language, the Way and the teachings of the ancient Sages, because they assume the form of specific acts of practice, will be all the more accessible on a linguistic level. But because it entails understanding the archaic language of a foreign people, understanding literary style is a formidable task.

114. Hōnen (1133–1212) is best known as the founder of the Pure Land (J. *jōdo*) sect of Buddhism in Japan. His teachings centered on the practice of *nembutsu,* the recitation of the name of Amida Buddha, an act that was thought to bring salvation to believers. Nichiren (1222–1282) was the founder of the Buddhist sect that is variously known as the Nichiren, Hokke, or Lotus sect. He favored the Lotus Sutra over all other Buddhist texts, called for the recitation of the phrase "I take refuge in the Lotus Sutra" (J. *namu myōhō renge kyō*), and was fiercely critical of rival sects, especially the Pure Land. At the outset Hōnen and Nichiren were followers of the Tendai sect, but both rejected its esoteric teachings for more accessible and thus more popular forms of religious practice.

Teachings of the Ch'eng Brothers and Chu Hsi

35. I now understand the gist of the question you have asked in two earlier letters. As for the methods of learning and the course to be followed, you will lose your way unless you have the guidance of those who are well versed in such matters. If what I am teaching you seems puzzling, it is best to keep asking about it. After making your inquiries, if you still do not understand, try practicing what you have learned. Or you might follow my teachings for a time even if you do not understand them and thus learn them in this way. In any event, if what I say proves to be wrong in the end, it is perfectly reasonable for you to reject it. Then again, I am not insisting that you follow my teachings.

Thanks to the inquiries you have sent from afar, I realize how intense your interest is in these matters. I have presented to both of you issues that are not treated in the works of the Ch'engs and Chu Hsi and that you have not encountered up to now, and your surprise is certainly to be expected. Now if you read just a little more widely, even without my prompting, you should begin to have doubts about the writings of the Ch'engs and Chu Hsi. Were I to present my ideas at this point, you would grasp them easily. There is a passage in the *Analects* that says: "The Master said, Only one who bursts with eagerness do I instruct; only one who bubbles with excitement do I enlighten. If I hold up one corner and a man cannot come back to me with the other three, I do not continue the lesson."[115] This is true not only of Confucius' school; contemporary pedagogies are exactly like this too. I am afraid this has something to do with the speed with which I have presented my ideas.

As for the notion that a new current appeared during the Sung dynasty, you seemed uncertain about this. The commentaries of the Ch'engs and Chu Hsi on the *Great Learning*, which you brought up, are incorrect. Consider, for example, the words "illumined virtue," the first tenet of the opening volume of the *Great Learning*.[116] In the *Tso Commentary*, there are the sayings "Yu's illumined virtue went great distances" and "He is a sage and possesses illumined virtue."[117]

115. *Lun-yü*, VII:8; Waley, *Analects*, p. 124.
116. *Ta-hsüeh*. The original reads: "The Way of the Great Learning exists in illuminating illumined virtue."
117. I have not been able to locate the sources of these passages.

These do not correspond at all with Chu Hsi's gloss on "illumined virtue." Moreover, the words "illumined virtue" frequently occur in the *Odes,* but do they accord with Chu Hsi's commentary?[118] My point here is that adding a theoretical dimension to these passages, as Chu Hsi did, should make them seem accessible, but truly understanding a literary style is a matter of understanding the felicity of its language. The scholarship presented in contemporary lectures is exceedingly argumentative and seems accessible, but it does not generate questions.

If one has not come to terms with the original text in its pristine form, one cannot claim to have mastered it. How can you speak of mastery without reading an unpunctuated edition on your own? Consider the eight-step section of the *Great Learning:* it is not part of the original text.[119] Specifically, note that "illuminating illumined virtue, loving the people, and abiding in the highest good" occurs at the beginning and the "investigation of things" at the end. Closing as it does with the single phrase "investigation of things," there is a flowing, falling movement from "when things are investigated and knowledge extended," to "when knowledge is extended, the will becomes sincere," down to "peace throughout the realm." The passage closes with "investigating things," and the various forms of practice mentioned before this—making the will sincere, rectifying the mind, and cultivating the personal life—are not very important. This is what a close reading of the text reveals.

Chu Hsi's gloss on "illuminating illumined virtue to the realm"

---

118. *Shih-ching,* III:1. The seventh stanza of this poem reads:
　　God said to King Wen,
　　"I am moved by your illumined virtue.
　　Your high renown has not made you put on proud airs,
　　Your greatness has not made you change former ways,
　　You do not try to be clever or knowing,
　　But follow God's precepts."
　　God said to King Wen,
　　"Take counsel with your partner states,
　　Unite with your brothers young and old,
　　And with your scaling ladders and siege platforms
　　Attack the castles of Ch'ung."
See Waley, *Book of Songs,* p. 258. I have substituted "illumined virtue" for "bright power," Waley's rendering of *ming te.*
　　119. Chu Hsi made much of this. See the preface to his *Commentary on the Great Learning (Ta-hsüeh chang-chü).*

goes on to say "causes all the people of the realm to illumine illuminated virtue."[120] Consider this objectively. I myself cannot believe that his notion of "having all the people of the realm illuminate illumined virtue" would have been possible even in the time of Yao and Shun. Chu Hsi separated the *Great Learning* and the *Lesser Learning* but never said that the *Great Learning* is something that all ordinary people should learn,[121] yet here he seems to be saying that the teachings of the *Great Learning* are to be taught to everyone in the realm. How can you not doubt things like this? Moreover, there is a passage in the *Mencius,* following a discussion of instruction, that reads: "When it is clear that those in authority understand human relationships, the people will be affectionate."[122] This is why it would be best not to change "becoming intimate with the people" to "renewing the people," as Chu Hsi does, because the phrase "renewing the people" refers to revolution in the *Book of History.* The teachings of the *Great Learning* deal with everyday affairs and are hardly what Chu Hsi makes them out to be. These are major discrepancies.

Moreover, there is a gloss in Chu Hsi's *Commentary on the Great Learning* on the two words "investigating things" that reads "exhaustively arriving at the principle of affairs and things."[123] It uses the words "exhausting principle" from the *Book of Changes* to gloss "investigating things." Chu Hsi's "exhaustively arriving at the principle of affairs and things" is not in the original text and adds the two words "exhausting principle"—thus producing a new meaning. How can one not have doubts about things like this? The phrase "exhausting principle" in the *Book of Changes* was a paean to the Sages for creating the changes and did not mean what present-day scholars believe it means. You should consider this objectively. Is the principle of the contemporary realm something that can be exhausted? Chu Hsi

120. Chu Hsi, *Ta-hsüeh huo-wen,* 10a. The passage in question reads: "The so-called 'illuminating illumined virtue in the realm' means to illuminate one's illumined virtue and to extend it so as to renovate the people and have them all illuminate their illumined virtue."

121. In his *Commentary on the Great Learning,* Chu Hsi wrote that "at the age of fifteen, everyone from imperial heirs and princes to the legitimate sons of dukes, viscounts, *and exceptional commoners* are to study the *Great Learning*" (my italics).

122. *Meng-tzu,* IIIA:3; Lau, *Mencius,* pp. 98–99.

123. See Chu Hsi's gloss on "investigating things" (C. *ke-wu*) in his *Commentary on the Great Learning.*

always discusses things that people do not normally do but will be forced to do. Moreover, in regard to the disposition of the detailed forms of practice presented in the discussion of the "three items" and in the "eight steps" sections, is it not true that they occur only in the *Great Learning* and not even once in the Six Classics? How can one not have misgivings?

The learning of the Ch'eng brothers and Chu Hsi is nothing more than the dichotomy of principle and material force, the division of heavenly principle and human desires, and the distinction between the original and physical natures. How is it that the ancient Sages ignored such fundamental matters? If the theories of the Ch'engs and Chu Hsi are correct, then it is obvious that they surpass Confucius. Then again, if the ancient Sages' teachings and methods are the standard, then are not the theories of the Ch'engs and Chu Hsi simply offshoots?

When the discussion comes to this point, the clever ones observe that the divergence of the Ch'engs and Chu Hsi from the teachings of the Sages has to do with differences in the nature of ages. They say this because they are unaware that it is ignorance of classical texts which allows them to assert that the past and the present are the same. The knowledge of the ancient Sages spanned past and present and even anticipated the various contemporary ills. Spanning past and present as they do, the ancient Sages' teachings are no less valuable for later ages than they were for antiquity. Were this not the case, they could not be called "sages."

The Sung Confucians' theory of principle and material force is reminiscent of the Buddhists' notion of an absolute reality and a provisional, phenomenal reality.[124] Their concept of "heavenly principle and human desire" echoes the Buddhists' "thusness" and "ignorance."[125] The terms "sage" and "worthy" did not exist in ancient times, and they resemble "buddha" and "bodhisattva."[126] Similarly,

---

124. Here Sorai uses the Buddhist terms *shintai* and *katai*. The former is the Japanese rendering of the Sanskrit *paramārtha*, which refers to absolute truth and the higher knowledge of the sage. The latter refers to the phenomenal world, a world of appearances and illusion, and originates in the doctrines of the Tendai sect.

125. "Thusness" (J. *shinnyo*) and "ignorance" (J. *mumyō*) are Mahayana terms. *Shinnyo* is the Japanese translation of the Sanskrit word *tathata*, the absolute reality. *Mumyō*, the ignorance of that absolute reality, is the Japanese rendering of *avidya*.

126. The word "bodhisattva" (J. *bosatsu*) referred, generally, to those who achieved Buddhist enlightenment. The Mahayana sects saw the bodhisattva as one

what is called the "transmission of orthodoxy" is not at all classical and resembles the Buddhists' "blood vessel transmission," nor is the idea of separating knowledge and action in one's teachings.[127] The Buddhists have what they call "interpretation" and "conduct."[128] The Sung Confucians' "suddenly achieving wide and far-reaching penetration" did not exist in ancient times and bears affinities to the Zen Buddhists' "great enlightenment" and "complete penetration."[129] And what they call "quiet sitting" is not classical but a mirror image of Zen meditation.[130]

---

who, though enlightened, chose not to become a buddha but to stay behind to help others achieve enlightenment and thus salvation.

127. *Kechimyaku sōden*, literally "blood vessel transmission," referred to the transmission of Buddhist teachings from a teacher to a disciple. The term was used by the esoteric sects and Zen Buddhists.

128. "Interpretation and conduct" is a translation of *gekō*, a compound that combines the graphs for "understanding" and "conduct."

129. "Suddenly achieving wide and far-reaching penetration" (C. *huo-jan kuan-t'ung*, J. *katsuzen kantsū*) appears at the end of Chu Hsi's gloss on the passage in the *Great Learning* that reads: "This is called knowing the root. This is called the perfecting of knowledge."

The meaning of the expression "The perfection of knowledge depends on the investigation of things" is this: If we wish to extend our knowledge to the utmost, we must investigate the principles of all things we come into contact with, for the intelligent mind of man is certainly formed to know, and there is not a single thing in which its principles do not inhere. It is only because all principles are not investigated that man's knowledge is incomplete. For this reason, the first step in the education of the adult is to instruct the learner, in regard to all things in the world, to proceed from what knowledge he has of their principles, and investigate further until he reaches the limit. After exerting himself in this way for a long time, he will *one day achieve a wide and far-reaching penetration*. Then the qualities of all things, whether internal or external, the refined or the coarse, will be apprehended, and the mind, in its total substance and great functioning, will be perfectly intelligent. This is called the investigation of things. This is called the perfection of knowledge.

See Chu Hsi, *Ta-hsüeh chang-chü*, chap. 5; Chan, *A Source Book in Chinese Philosophy*, p. 89; the italics are mine.

"Great enlightenment" (C. *ta-wu*, J. *ōsatori*) and "complete penetration" (C. *ch'e-ti*, J. *tettei*) are Zen Buddhist terms that describe the deepest kind of spiritual awakening.

130. Sorai is right about "quiet sitting" (C. *ching-tso*, J. *seiza*). Neo-Confucian philosophers adopted it as a method of self-cultivation despite its obvious Buddhist and Taoist origins. In fact, Chu Hsi spoke of giving over "half the day to book learning and the other half to quiet sitting." The point is that it was a means of spiritual cultivation.

As far as the original and physical natures are concerned, you should discuss them as fully as you can.[131] In the end it all comes down to the physical nature and that alone. Moreover, the idea of transforming the physical nature is the height of absurdity, as it forces people to do what they cannot do. If you reflect objectively on whether there are things that you can or cannot do today and whether something could or could not have existed in the past, then the Sung Confucians' errors should be apparent.

You stated that one cannot penetrate the inner recesses of the sagely classics without Chu Hsi's new commentaries. You say this because you believe that you mastered the classics with the help of these commentaries. Yet Chu Hsi's glosses are like his discussions of "illumined virtue" and "investigating things," which I discussed earlier. They diverge from the classical language and thus would hardly do as a ladder to the sagely classics. Moreover, his ideas of "principle" and "material force," the "original" and "physical" natures, and "heavenly principle and human desire" are not found in the teachings of the ancient Sages. Neither are his methods of cultivation: "dividing knowledge and action," "investigating things," "extending knowledge," "making the thoughts sincere," "rectifying the mind," and "maintaining seriousness." This is why his commentaries cannot serve as a ladder to the sagely classics. You should know that if you speak in this way, you will not know what to do.

With the original texts alone, you will understand very little. It might be good to start with texts that deal with affairs whose principles are not very deep—texts like the *Tso Commentary, Records of the Historian,* and *History of the Former Han.* As you read them, you will get used to their style and their meaning, and later, when you turn to the Six Classics, you will be able to handle even the original texts alone.

At this point I should relate my tale of past sins. I owe my knowl-

---

131. The distinction between an "original nature" (C. *pen-jan chih hsing,* J. *honzen no sei*) and a "physical nature" (C. *ch'i-chih chih hsing,* J. *kishitsu no sei*) was a cardinal Neo-Confucian concept with obvious Taoist and Buddhist echoes. The question of human nature had been a concern of Confucian philosophers since Mencius advanced his theory that human nature is innately good, and Ch'eng I and Chu Hsi further refined the concept. Sorai is probably referring to the latter's formulation.

edge of the classics to Kenbyō.[132] Here is what happened: Kenbyō ordered me to see how good a group of pages were at reading the Four Books and Five Classics.[133] So that summer, day after day, every day, I had the young men sit across from me and read out loud. At first I scolded them for their lapses, but because we were at this every day from six in the morning to four in the afternoon, rising only to eat and to relieve ourselves, we gradually exhausted ourselves, and even my inclination to examine them disappeared. After a while the person reading out loud simply recited, and I was shocked to discover that even I, the examiner, was just staring at the text. In the beginning I turned the pages as the young men read, but after a while I no longer bothered, and the examiner and the readers did not stay together. We did, however, live for a time with the original texts and in this way divorced ourselves from the commentaries. Without really knowing what we were doing, we looked at and read the original texts alone, and while staring at them in a daze, doubts arose first on one point, then on another, and these became the seeds of discovery. We now realize that this is what is meant by studying the classics. The understanding that one quickly attains by relying on commentaries seems to have some value, yet there is no self-discovery. This is my tale of past sins.

This is why I have my students do what I suggested that you do. But it is precisely because I have read as widely as I can, as I said earlier, that I am able to read and understand the classics in the original. If you do not read broadly, you will never be able to leave behind what you have learned from Chu Hsi's commentaries. Although reading broadly may seem not to have anything to do with the classics, there is what might be called the utility of nonutility; gain and profit are to be found in unexpected places.

I realize that you have doubts about the Way's being neither the "principle of how things and affairs should be" nor the "natural way

132. Kenbyō was the posthumous name of the fifth shogun, Tokugawa Tsunayoshi, who ruled from 1680 to 1709 and was the patron of Sorai's employer, Yanagisawa Yoshiyasu.
133. Pages (J. *koshōgumi*) had been a fixture at the shogun's court since the fourteenth century. In Sorai's time, there were several hundred pages organized into fifty-man units, serving as the shogun's personal attendants, bodyguards, and, when he left the palace, as his runners.

of heaven and earth," but simply the way created by the Sages and a method of governing the provinces and the realm. Given that you are mired in Sung learning, this is understandable. First, the "natural way of heaven and earth" is the theory of Lao-tzu and Chuang-tzu.[134] They came up with the idea that a pristine heaven and earth, just as they are, with absolutely nothing added, comprise the way, which sounds truly wonderful and conclusive. But if you follow this theory through to its logical end, it does not lead to the destruction of the Way of the Sages, and thus is illogical. And the theory of the "principle of how things and affairs should be" was based on the idea of the natural way of heaven and earth. All these theories are products of their creators' fulsome confidence and their shallow faith in the ancient Sages.

When the Sung Confucians carry out what they call "investigating things" and "extending knowledge," they decide at the start that such and such a matter should be like this and such and such a matter like that and assert that this is no different from the Way of the Sages. This is a narrow view. Caught up in the growth of their own knowledge, they do not realize that many of the things that they initially thought should be disposed in a certain way cannot be so disposed. They think like someone reaching quickly for the handle of a sword and thus produce this kind of knowledge. The Way of the Sages is extraordinarily deep, broad, and large; it is hardly the sort of affair that appears when scholars, relying on their own knowledge, say that such and such a principle should exist. Thinking smugly, "Ah, yes, this, of course, is how I expect things should be," and feeling that it is we who grant seals of approval to the Sages is the height of impudence. Moreover, when one proceeds, without thinking, to fit the Way of the Sages to the measure of one's own mind and thinks, "Ah, yes, this, of course, is how I expect things should be," one ends up accepting only what corresponds to one's thinking and discarding the rest as unreasonable. One may believe that this is the Way of the Sages, but it is simply one's own construction. As one acquires more and more of this kind of knowledge, one's own knowledge becomes shallow and crude, and the depth, breadth, and magnitude of the Way of the Sages

134. The phrase "natural way of heaven and earth" (C. *t'ien-ti tzu-jan chih tao*, J. *tenchi shizen no michi*) does not occur in either the *Lao-tzu* or *Chuang-tzu*. It does correspond, however, to the Taoist identification of the way and "nature" (C. *tzu-jan*, J. *shizen*).

become increasingly remote as the days pass; in the end, one's arrogance will be a thing to behold.

Moreover, the words "the principle of how things and affairs should be" can be applied to almost anything. In the tea ceremony, flower arranging, *waka* composition, calligraphy, and fencing, even in the Ogasawara style of etiquette, the wearing of formal dress, and the way long and short swords are drawn, there are conventions dictating just how things should be done. Should all these arts be construed as the Way of the Sages? Imagining that the same principle runs through the myriad things and identifying the various arts I just mentioned with the Way of the Sages is truly, one should say, a gross error.

I myself simply believe deeply in the Sages. So, for example, even if there is something that I know should not be, if it implicates the Way of the Sages, I assume that it cannot be that unhappy an affair and carry it out. After carrying it out, "it will become, through repeated practice, one's nature" and "what is practiced will be like one's heaven-endowed nature," and it will feel as though one were going down a great road.[135]

I have already spoken of the Way as the creation of the Sages. At the center of the Way are the Five Relations. Of these Five Relations, the love of a father and son is natural. Showing respect for one's elder brother is something on which one's parents insist from the time one is little, and thus one is well aware of it. Those who have never had this instruction, on the other hand, know nothing about revering their elder brothers. The relationship of husbands and wives is the way established by the Sage Fu Hsi. In the world of antiquity, people lived as animals and came to know the way of rulers and subjects and the way of friends only after the Sages created them.

The Sages, using their extraordinarily deep, broad, and great knowledge, created the ways of social relations in accordance with the innate endowment of humans, and in this way the human world was established. Thus, when one realizes that even those who have

---

135. The first passage is from the *Shu-ching*, Tai-chia shang. The original reads: "The king was not yet able to change his course. E Yin said to himself, 'This is real unrighteousness, and is becoming by practice second nature.'" See Legge, CC, III:203. The second passage compresses two passages in the *School Sayings of Confucius (Kung-tzu chia-yu):* "If there is a little development, then it will be like the heavenly nature" and "When it becomes a habit, it will be like nature." See *Kung-tzu chia-yu*, Ch'i-shih er-ti tzu-chieh.

not studied the Way generally have little trouble understanding the Five Relations, the Five Relations will seem like part of the original human endowment. For example, the cultivation of the five grains was initiated by Shen Nung. The construction of buildings and the weaving of garments was the work of Huang Ti. Inasmuch as these innovations as well were created in accordance with human nature, they have spread throughout the world and people regard them as given and natural. The same is true with the way of the Five Relations. The benevolence of the ancient Sages is so broad, great, and infinite that the breadth and greatness of their virtue equals heaven and earth, and people's not being aware of it is like their not knowing the benevolence of heaven and earth, the sun and the moon. The saying in *A Lost History of Chou* that "he whose virtue matches heaven and earth is to be called an emperor" is making the same point.[136] If one thinks carefully about these matters, one should see that describing the Way as "the principle of how things and affairs should be" is like declaring that the Sages are one's disciples.

Tzu Ssu was speaking of all these things created in accordance with human nature when he said, "To follow our nature is called the way."[137] "Cultivating the way is called instruction" refers to studying the Way.[138] Because the Way is broad, great, and infinite, it will elude the grasp of even those intent on studying it. The guidelines that make the Way manageable and easy to learn are called "instruction." Describing the governing of province and realm as "instruction" is a misnomer and is not found in the Six Classics or the *Analects*. The Sung Confucians, with their philosophy of principle, use logic to make the specious claim that government is a species of instruction. Despite its familiarity, principle is a Sung Confucian invention and is not found in ancient texts. You should see the word "instruction" as always opposed to "study."

136. *A Lost History of Chou* is a mysterious text whose provenance is uncertain. It was probably written late in the Eastern Chou (771–221 B.C.) period.

137. *Chung-yung*, 1. The relevant section in the original reads: "What Heaven imparts to humans is called human nature. To follow our nature is called the Way. Cultivating the Way cannot be separated from us for a moment. What can be separated from us is not the Way." See Chan, *A Source Book in Chinese Philosophy*, p. 98. I have altered Chan's translation slightly.

138. *Chung-yung*, 1. This, too, is from the opening passage of the the *Doctrine of the Mean*.

As for your not understanding that the methods of governing the realm and province comprise the Way, you are still mired in Sung learning, which is why you see things as you do. First of all, the founders of my Way are Yao and Shun, who were Sons of Heaven. Those of their successors designated as "sages" were Yu, T'ang, Wen, Wu, and the Duke of Chou—all of whom governed the realm and country; and Confucius transmitted their Way. Thus the Way of the Sages is solely a way for governing the realm and country, and things like ritual, music, punishments, and administration comprise the Way. Consider the passage in the *Analects* that finds Confucius visiting the walled town of Wu where Tzu Yu was a minister and laughing when he heard the "sound of stringed instruments and singing." Tzu Yu responded, "A gentleman who has studied the Way will be all the tenderer toward his fellow humans; a commoner who has studied the Way will be all the easier to employ."[139] Clearly music is being spoken of as the Way. Because Tzu Yu was a direct disciple of Confucius, terminological variation is impossible. The Sung Confucians' commentaries contain no clarification of the word "way" as it occurs in this passage, and Chu Hsi also is silent.[140] As for the so-called Five Relations, had they not been instituted, the realm never would have been governed, which is why the Sages created them. The Way of the Sages, in the final analysis, was created to pacify the realm and country.

As for self-cultivation, those who do not cultivate themselves will not have the respect or trust of their underlings, nor will they be able to carry out the Way. This is why Gentlemen cultivate themselves. If contemporary scholars understood this and recognized the Way of the Sages as a way to govern the realm and country, it would be like holding the Six Classics in the palms of their hands. The perspective of latter-day Confucians is shallow, however, and they lack talent. No

---

139. *Lun-yü*, XVII:4. The original reads:
When the Master went to the walled town of Wu, he heard the sound of stringed instruments and singing. Our Master said with a gentle smile, "To kill a chicken one does not use an ox-cleaver." Tzu-yu replied saying, I remember once hearing you say, "A gentleman who has studied the Way will be all the tenderer towards his fellow-men; a commoner who has studied the Way will be all the easier to employ." The Master said, "My disciples, what he says is quite true. What I said just now was only meant as a joke." See Waley, *Analects*, pp. 208–210.

140. See Chu Hsi's gloss on *Lun-yü*, XVII:4, in his *Lun-yü chi-chu*, and see Sorai's comment in his commentary on the *Lun-yü, Rongochō, NMSCZ*, VII:316–317.

matter what the issue, they think of it solely in terms of themselves. As a result, their methods of spiritual cultivation and their theories have flourished, leading them to try to become sages using contemporary forms of cultivation. Their belief that if one becomes a sage the realm and country will be governed naturally has led them into Buddhist and Taoist modes of thinking, although of course they differ on certain points. Buddha's was a world of beggars, and he was without a family, a wife, children, a province, or a realm—as a result, his way was exclusively an affair of the self. These views diverge from the general outline of the Way of the Sages.

Before Ti K'u, who was Huang Ti's great-grandson, rulers used virtue to govern the realm.[141] Yao and Shun created the Way for the first time, which is why Confucius transmitted their legacy. The fact that the *Book of History* begins with Yao and Shun is because they were the original founders of my Way. Had Yao and Shun used virtue to govern the realm, they never would have created the Way. For ages without sages and worthies but with the transmission of the Way, they devised and established the means by which the realm and the country could be governed as though there were sages and worthies. And Yu, T'ang, Wen, and the Duke of Chou modified what they inherited from Yao and Shun. Thus if Confucius had not studied the past, he would not have known the Way.

The Sung Confucians know how to govern the realm only by means of virtue; they do not know the Way. Accordingly, when they speak of Confucius' "love of learning" or "studying widely," their glosses are not very lucid.[142] They leave it unclear whether Confucius is being self-effacing or merely enticing scholars to delve more deeply. They use their own ideas to assess the Sages and fail to grasp the profound truth of the Sage Confucius' words.

Knights are the ones who assist rulers and help them govern the provinces and realm. Because of this, their ignorance of the Way of the Sages makes it hard for them to escape the charge that they are

141. Ti K'u was the great-grandson of Huang Ti, one of the mythical rulers of ancient China and one of those that Sorai designated a Sage. He is said to have assisted Chuan Hsu, Huang Ti's grandson, and later to have replaced him as emperor.

142. Sorai is alluding to *Lun-yü*, II:14, V:28, VI:3, XI:7, XIX:5, XIX:6. The editors of *Nihon no meicho* offer a different reading of this passage. See *Nihon no meicho*, 16:353.

salary stealers, and this is why they study the Way. You should see that they are without the kind of self-indulgence that transforms a person into a buddha or sage. Moreover, if one were to declare that the provinces and realm will be governed naturally only when a ruler becomes a sage and then to help one's ruler become a sage, the days and years would pass, and when would the provinces and realm be pacified and governed? Even the criticism that Sung Confucians have "substance" but not "function" points to errors in their scholarly methods that cannot be overlooked. You should think carefully about this.

In the end, the rejection of the idea that governing the provinces and realm is the Way encourages the view that ritual, music, performance, and titles are the crude remains of the past and that the Way is highly refined and delicate. The Way is neither refined nor coarse, neither root nor branch: "It has one thread running through it."[143] And valuing the refined and slighting the crude is a residue of Buddhist and Taoist influence. This is an important distinction.

Your query about whether the Sung Confucians, despite their loss of the ancient language, had principles that were universal and spanned both past and present is absurd. Those who have lost the ancient language have departed from the principle of the original texts. If all you can say about the Sung Confucians' divergence from the principles of the original texts is that their "principle is universal," you are exhibiting the worst kind of partisanship.

You asked whether practicing reading unpunctuated texts as monks read sutras was all right. You are free to do as you like and to read texts—whether or not they are punctuated—in any one of several ways. Your regarding this as the most difficult matter of the moment is true. If you rely on punctuated texts, however, your scholarship will never progress. It would be good for you to read unpunctuated texts that are easy to read: histories, the *Five Assorted Offerings,* even medical or military texts, or whatever.[144]

143. *Lun-yü,* IV:15. The entire passage reads: "The Master said, 'Shen! My Way has one thread that runs right through it.' Master Tseng said, 'Yes.' When the Master had gone out, the disciples asked, saying 'What did he mean?' Master Tseng said, 'Our Master's Way is simply this: Loyalty, consideration.'" See Waley, *Analects,* p. 105.

144. *Five Assorted Offerings (Wu Tsa Tsu)* was written by the Ming scholar Hsieh Chao-che (1567–1624) and treats cosmological and human affairs.

Your wanting to translate Hayashi Gahō's *One View of the Five Ages* into classical Chinese is fine; but before you do this, read Chinese histories.[145] Translating it into Chinese with only what you know now would not have any value.

I am suggesting that you stop studying Sung Confucianism for four reasons: first, for the sake of your reading; second, for the sake of your literary style; third, for the sake of your study of the classics; and fourth, for the sake of your character. Sung Confucianism is doing you great harm in these four areas.

First, what I mean by "for the sake of your reading" is this: The reading of texts begins with the reading of ancient texts. Chu Hsi's new commentaries did not exist from antiquity up through the T'ang dynasty, and even during the Sung dynasty there were books that did not use his new commentaries. Thus, when using Chu Hsi's commentaries in reading the classics, one discovers that his interpretations of certain passages in the classics differ from those found elsewhere. This is why your familiarity with Sung Confucianism will keep you from mastering texts written before T'ang and Sung. This is what I mean when I say that your study of Sung Confucianism will not help your reading.

Second, when I say that you should stop studying Sung Confucianism "for the sake of your literary style," what I have in mind is the following: If there are two types of literary style—the descriptive and the argumentative—then all Sung Confucian texts are argumentative and not descriptive. Although description is the stuff of literary style, you are unable to write in the descriptive style, owing to the influence of Sung Confucian texts. Moreover, the Sung Confucians' literary style is reminiscent of *kana* written with Chinese characters. Their language lacks elegance and is full of vulgar characters. As a result, when you master this style your writing will change, and no matter how much you practice, your writing will resemble commentaries and you will be unable to write in a truly literary style. This will be detrimental to your literary style.

Third, when I suggest that you stop studying Sung Confucianism

145. Hayashi Gahō (1618–1680) was the third son of the pioneering Neo-Confucian scholar and teacher Hayashi Razan, and like his father he served the Tokugawa in various official capacities. He also completed *Comprehensive Mirror of Our Nation's Dynasty (Honchō tsugan),* the multivolume history of Japan that the Tokugawa ordered his father to write.

because of the "unhappy effect it is having on your study of the classics," I am thinking of what I said earlier: It is because the Sung Confucians lost the ancient language that the meaning of the classics is different. They added notions like "principle," "material force," "heavenly principle," "human desire," and so forth, which impose a new layer of meaning on the Way of the Sages. Generally, Sung Confucian scholars do not interpret the writings of the ancient Sages in terms of their apparent meaning. The Ch'eng brothers and Chu Hsi were brilliant and extraordinary men who departed from the texts of the ancient Sages and came up with their own perspective on the classics. Thus, following the Sung Confucians in pursuit of the Way of the ancient Sages is like pointing the yoke of one's cart south when one wants to go north. This is what I mean when I say that Sung Confucianism will have "an unhappy effect on your study of the classics."

It is for these many reasons that I called Sung Confucianism a "harmful friend."[146] When you finally have your own perspective and a modicum of learning, nothing, no matter what, will be difficult. But when you reach this point, you will detest the writings of the Sung Confucians. At the moment, you still are attached to them, and this is why you ask what you do. Those nurtured on their commentaries on the classics sharply distinguish right and wrong, heterodox and orthodox; they want everything handled efficiently from beginning to end; and they often are arrogant. Many condemn elegance and literary finesse and have wretched personalities. You have probably heard the rumors about the character of Yamazaki Ansai and Asami Keisai.[147] The problem is not just their unfortunate pedagogy; it has to do with the one-sidedness of the Sung Confucians' approach. Ordinary folk say that scholars have foul dispositions, and this is not far off the mark.

As you both will hear much about governing—this as a matter of your birthright—I want you to escape the harm that Sung Confucianism can bring. Generally, the Sung Confucian way of learning elevates the mind, and so if you have the deepest regard for the Ch'engs and Chu Hsi, you should end up wanting to become as great as they were. The Ch'engs and Chu Hsi studied the classics on their own, without relying on others' work, and in time achieved their great status. One cannot duplicate the achievement of the Ch'engs and Chu Hsi by

146. *Lun-yü*, XVI:4.
147. Asami Keisai (1652–1711) was one of Yamazaki Ansai's leading disciples.

studying what they left behind. If, after engaging in the broadest kind of inquiry and studying, as the Ch'engs and Chu Hsi did, you still see their theories in a positive light, then at that point it would be all right to employ those theories. Your current belief and faith in the Ch'engs and Chu Hsi reflect what you have heard. In my school we usually do not rely on others but look closely at the writings of the ancient Sages.

I understand that several of you are reading the *Book of Odes* and the *Book of History*. I think this is wonderful. In Confucius' time, there was nothing else besides the *Odes* and *History*. The *Analects*, *Mencius*, and *Book of Rites* quote from these two texts but not others. All one sees is "The *Odes* says . . . " and "The *History* says . . . . " When you study the *Odes* and *History*, you are studying just as the ancients did, and this is truly commendable.

You indicated that the new commentaries are all you have. This being the case, I think that even with the new commentaries you will manage to master the meaning of the original texts. Because Chu Hsi's *Collected Commentaries on the Book of Odes* is not the best of his writings, it will do little harm.[148] The new commentary on the *Book of History* by Chu Hsi's disciple Ts'ai Ch'en is a mindless piece of work.[149] You would do well to read Ch'en Shih-k'ai's *A Companion to Mr. Ts'ai's Commentary on the Book of History* and Huang Chen-ch'eng's *An Encyclopedia of the Book of History*. As for the *Book of Odes*, Ho K'ai's *Ancient Meanings of the Book of Odes* would be good, but Japanese editions are not available. At the very least, you should look at Ku Meng-lin's *A Primer on the Book of Odes*.

As for the Sung Confucians' treatment of the *Book of Odes*, let me list their most egregious errors. The statement in Chu Hsi's preface to *Collected Commentaries of the Book of Odes* that "poetry exists to praise the good and condemn the evil" is a great misconception.[150] If "poetry exists only to praise the good and condemn the evil," there

148. The correct title of Chu Hsi's work is *Shih chi-ch'uan*. The *NRI* edition gives *Shih-ching chu-ch'uan* as the title of this work, and this is obviously an error. The *Nihon no meicho* edition, which changes it to *Shih-ching chi-ch'uan*, also may be in error. See *NRI*, 6:201 and *Nihon no meicho*, 16:356.

149. Ts'ai Ch'en was one of Chu Hsi's disciples and wrote a commentary on the *Book of History* entitled *Collected Transmissions of the Book of History (Shu-ching chi-ch'uan)*.

150. See Chu Hsi's preface to his *Shih-ching chi-ch'uan*, *Ssu-pu pei-yao*, Ching, shih-lei.

should be a slightly better method of doing this. I have never heard of anyone using poetry "to praise the good and condemn the evil." Based on my knowledge of the ancient Sages, I would say that something as unpersuasive as this simply cannot be. After all, the *Book of Odes* contains a number of erotic poems. Chu Hsi's commentary suggests that these poems are included in the *Odes* so that evil can be condemned, but one should say that, rather, they serve to guide the depraved. You should think very carefully about these issues.

You seem not to have mastered the *Book of Odes,* not even in your dreams. In the *Analects,* one finds the following passages: "Unless you study the *Odes* you will be ill equipped to speak" and "If a man who knows the three hundred odes by heart ... proves incapable of exercising his own initiative when sent to foreign states, then what use are the *Odes* to him?"[151] These passages are saying that poetry is a means of teaching one about language. As for truly understanding human nature, if one does not achieve that understanding by means of what the *Book of Odes* teaches, the poems in the *Odes* will be concrete forms that are never expressed."[152]

The Sung Confucians are trapped by their conceptions of right and wrong, heterodox and orthodox, and pay no attention to the discussions of the *Book of Odes* in the *Analects* and the Sages' utterances. Their seeing things as right and wrong, heterodox and orthodox, may originate in their praising and blaming. I am telling you all of this because you should know the gist of the *Book of Odes* before you read it. There is absolutely no difference between the poetry of the

---

151. *Lun-yü,* XVI:13 and XIII:5; Lau, *Analects,* pp. 141, 119.

152. Although "concrete form" is not the usual rendering of *mono* (C. *wu*), it approximates Sorai's usage in this instance. As he explained in *Distinguishing Names,* "concrete form" referred to the "particulars of a teaching," which provided "guidelines" for self-cultivation. Sorai believed that when one had practiced classical Chinese etiquette and ritual to the point of mastery and had absorbed the diction of classical Chinese verse, one attained concrete form. He wrote: "When one has grown accustomed to practicing a ceremonial form by performing it for some time and succeeded in retaining it, this is called the 'coming of *concrete form.*'" And: "In expressing one's views, one should never blurt them out impulsively or choose one's words capriciously. Instead, one should memorize and use to express one's thoughts the ancient words that have been transmitted from the past and survive in the cosmos. When one memorizes these ancient words and has them in mind, it is as though one actually has *concrete form.*" See Sorai, *Benmei, NST,* 36:253–254; the italics are mine. See also *Bendō, NST,* 36:205, *Benmei, NST,* 36:238, and *Gakusoku, NRI,* 6:123.

Book of Odes and that of later generations, and it is fine to see the
Odes simply as poetry.

Administrative Documents

You asked about the language of administrative documents. If you
have not read works like the *Governmental Encyclopedia* and statutes and codes, you will not master this issue.[153] Each dynasty in Chinese history has brought about changes in its institutions and laws.
Each set of changes represents the conception of the dynastic founder,
and social organization as a whole is affected, as are institutions and
laws. Those who are unaware of this will not understand the affairs
of particular periods, and even though they read history, they will
never master it. In the case of the classics of the Three Dynasties,
nothing will be clear without some mastery of the *Rites of Chou,* the
Rites of Yi, and the *Book of Rites.* As for ancient Japan, one will not
understand our aristocratic age without examining the administrative
and legal codes of that time and the *Procedures of the Engi Era.*[154]
Thus, if one is aware of the institutional changes that occurred in the
various Chinese dynasties and in ancient Japan as well, one will recognize that contemporary institutions differ from those of China on
some points and from those of Japan's aristocratic age on other
points, and contemporary political affairs will be crystal clear. Those
who read only things like Chu Hsi's *Commentaries on the Four Books*
and *Reflections on Things at Hand*—the texts of the philosophy of
principle—will be unaware of these institutional differences and,
when they discuss these issues, will simply pay lip service to what they
do not understand.

153. The *Governmental Encyclopedia (T'ung Tien)* is a two-hundred-volume
work compiled during the T'ang dynasty that dealt with all variety of administrative matters. It is divided into eight sections: currency, selection of officials,
bureaucratic offices, ritual, music, military, punishments, and defense. The
statutes and codes that Sorai mentions here were those enacted by the state in
China.

154. The *Procedures of the Engi Era (Engi-shiki)* is a fifty-volume collection of
government regulations compiled between 905 and 927 as a supplement to the
broader-gauged administrative and legal codes formulated on T'ang models—the
Ōmi, Asuka Kiyomihara, Taihō, and Yōrō codes. It supplies detailed instructions
about everything from festivals and ceremonies to bureaucratic practice. It is the
third such supplementary collection.

In this connection, I will mention that the saying "a peck of rice and three cash" indicated that the T'ang emperor T'ai-tsung's government was good and the realm well governed.[155] It actually means that a peck of rice sold for three cash.[156] Recently, owing to a slight drop in the price of rice, warriors, townspeople, and farmers have all been impoverished. What do you think of these differences? They tell us that institutional differences spawn variations in the patterns in the world at large. As for your question about the language of administrative documents, I think you are noticing the right things.

Composing Poetry

I think your wanting to compose poetry is a fine idea. The poetry of antiquity and that of later generations are the same phenomenon. If one has never composed poetry, one can never master the *Book of Odes*.

Wide Learning

Your reading the *Songs of Ch'u* and the *Conversations from the States* is an extraordinarily good idea. Your reading the *Spring and Autumn Annals of the House of Lü, Huai Nan-tzu, School Sayings of Confucius, Intrigues from the Warring States, Lao-tzu, Chuang-tzu,* and *Lieh-tzu* is also commendable. As a way of broadening one's knowledge and perspective, "wide learning" is essential—even Confucius spoke of it. And the distaste of modern practitioners of the philosophy of principle for what they call "miscellaneous learning" runs against the Sages' words. One might see them as being of the same ilk as the Nichiren sect.

---

155. T'ai-tsung was the posthumous name of Li Shih-min (600–649), founder of the T'ang dynasty (618–906). In 617 he persuaded his father, Li Yuan, to defy the ruler of the Sui dynasty (589–617), and after a series of battles with other rebels and contenders for power, the Li forces prevailed and established a new dynasty. Li Shih-min succeeded his father in 626 and reigned until his death in 649. Like many dynastic founders, he is remembered for his military prowess, administrative skill, and magnanimity.

156. A *to,* or "peck," is a unit of volume or capacity equal to approximately 4.76 U.S. gallons; one *to* is one-tenth of one *koku.* A *mon,* or "cash," is a metal coin made of copper, iron, or brass with a stamped-out center.

Final Thoughts

You inquired about my book *Distinguishing the Way*. In fact, there are two books, *Distinguishing the Way* and *Distinguishing Names*. As for my responses to your queries, my having to forgo my other duties, owing to gastrointestinal problems, has been a boon, and I was able to respond as I did. Later, when I am busier, detailed responses will be impossible. You might reread my responses for half a year or so, studying and practicing what I have suggested. After that, if you think that what I have said makes sense and you want to follow my methods and engage in scholarship, I will have a bookseller make copies of *Distinguishing the Way* and *Distinguishing Names* and send them to you. If you do not do this, I believe that you will encourage disagreement and fail to make progress.

GLOSSARY

Abe Yoshio 阿部吉雄

agemai 上米

Asaka Tanpaku 安積澹泊

Asami Keisai 浅見絅斎

Ashikaga Takauji 足利尊氏

Asuka Kiyomihara 飛鳥淨御原

Baba Nobuharu, 馬場信春，

　Nobukatsu 　信勝

bakufu 幕府

Bendō 弁道

Benmei 弁名

Bitō Masahide 尾藤正英

Bokumon Gakuha 木門学派

bosatsu 菩薩

Chan Kuo-tse 戰國策

Chang Tsai 張載

ch'e-ti / tettei 徹底

ch'en-pi / chinbi 陳皮

Ch'en Shih-k'ai 陳師凱

Ch'eng 成

Ch'eng Hao 程顥

Ch'eng I 程頤

ch'i-chih chih 氣質之性

　hsing / kishitsu

　no sei

ch'i-ts'ai / kisai 棄才

ch'i-wu / kibutsu 棄物

ch'iao-yen ling-se 巧言令色

Chichibu Shigetada 秩父重忠

chien 健

ch'ien / kan 乾

chih / chi 智

chih-chih / chi o itasu 致知

Ch'in 秦

Chin-ssu lu 近思錄

ching / ido 井

ch'ing / nasake 情

ching-tso / seiza 靜坐

Chou 周

Chou-li 周礼

Chou Pi 周弼

Chou Tun-i 周敦頤

Ch'u 楚

Chu Hsi 朱熹

Chu-ke Kung-ming 諸葛孔明

Ch'u-tz'u 楚辞

Ch'u Yüan 屈原

Chuang Tzu 莊子

chün / gun 郡

Ch'un-ch'iu 春秋

chün-tzu / kunshi	君子	*Hanshi jiten*	藩史事典
Chung-yung	中庸	Hattori Nankaku	服部南郭
Chung-yung chang-chü	中庸章句	Hayashi	林
		Hayashi Gahō	林鵞峯
Daigakukai	大学解	Hayashi Razan	林羅山
daikan	代官	Hikita Tatewaki	疋田帯刀
Dazai Shundai	太宰春台	Hikita Yakara	疋田族
Dōgen	道元	Hino Tatsuo	日野龍夫
Dōjimon	童子問	Hiraishi Naoaki	平石直昭
Edo	江戸	Ho Ching-ming, Ta-fu	何景明, 大復
Edo jidai	江戸時代		
Engi-shiki	延喜式	Ho K'ai	何楷
fa / hō	法	Honda Tadamune	本多忠統
fa-ming / hatsumei	発明	Hōnen	法然
fang-hsiao / hōkō	放効	Honnō	本納
Fang Hui	方回	Hori Keizan	堀景山
Fu Hsi	伏羲	Hoshina Masayuki	保科正之
fu-tzu / fushi	附子	*Hou-han shu*	後漢書
fudai	譜代	*hsi / narau*	習 / 習う
Fujiwara Seika	藤原惺窩	Hsia	夏
Gakusoku	学則	*hsiang-yüan*	郷愿
gekō	解行	Hsiao T'ung	蕭統
Genroku jidai	元禄時代	Hsieh Chao-che	謝肇淛
giji shushigaku	疑似朱子学	*hsien / ken*	県
go	碁	Hsü Hsing	許行
Go-Toba tennō	後鳥羽天皇	*hsün-chieh / kunkai*	勲階
gundai	郡代	Hsün-tzu	荀子
hakaru	計る	Hu Yüan	胡瑗
Han	漢	*Huai Nan-tzu*	淮南子
Han Fei Tzu	韓非子	*huan-ku*	換骨
Han Hsin	韓信	Huang Chen-ch'eng	黄鎮成
Han Yü	韓愈		
Hanbe Ansu	伴部安崇	Huang Shan-ku, T'ing-chien	黄山谷, 庭堅
Hanshi daijiten	藩史大事典		

Huang Ti	黄帝	*Ken'en zuihitsu*	蘐園隨筆
huo-jan kuan-	豁然貫通	*ketsumyaku sōden*	血脈相伝
t'ung / katsuzen		Kimon Gakuha	崎門学派
kantsū		Kitajima	北島正元
hyō	俵	Masamoto	
I-ching	易經	*kobunjigaku*	古文辞学
Imanaka Kanshi	今中寛司	*kogakuha*	古学派
Inoue Tetsujirō	井上哲次郎	*koku*	石
Itō Jinsai	伊藤仁齋	Kōsaka Toratsuna	高坂虎綱
Iwanami kōza	岩波講座日本	*Kōyō gunkan*	甲陽軍鑑
nihon rekishi	歴史	Ku Meng-lin	顧夢麟
jen / hito	人	Kuan Shu	管叔
jen / jin	仁	*Kuan-tzu*	管子
jen-ch'e / jinja	仁者	Kun	鯀
jen-yü / jinyoku	人欲	*Kung-tzu chia-yü*	孔子家語
jitsugaku	実学	Kuo T'o-t'o	郭橐駝
jōdo	淨土	Kusunoki	楠木正成
jōmen	定免	Masashige	
kan-ts'ao / kansō	甘草	*kyōgen*	狂言
kana	仮名	Kyōhō	亨保
kanamono	仮名物	Lao-tzu	老子
kang	剛	*li / ri*	里
Kansan yoroku	閑散余録	*Li-chi*	礼記
kasuru	化する	Li Ching	李靖
katai	仮諦	Li Meng-yang,	李夢陽,空同
Katō Daini	加藤大貳	Kung-t'ung	
Kayabachō	茅場町	Li P'an-lung, Yü-lin	李攀竜,于鱗
Kazusa	上総	Li Shih-min	李世民
ke-wu / kakubutsu	格物	Li Ssu	李斯
kemi	檢見	Li T'ung	李侗
Kemmu	建武	Li-yüan	李淵
Kenbyō	憲廟	Liang	梁
Ken'en-juku	蘐園塾	Lieh-tzu	列子
Ken'en zatsuwa	蘐園雜話	Lin Hsi-yi	林希逸

liu-kuan / rokkan	六官	*namu myōhō renge*	南無妙法蓮
liu-pu / rokubu	六部	*kyō*	華経
Liu Tsung-yüan	柳宗元	*Nan-ching*	難経
Lo Ch'in-shun	羅欽順	*nembutsu*	念仏
Lü-shih chun-ch'iu	呂氏春秋	Nemoto Sonshi	根本遜志
Lü Tsu-ch'ien	呂祖謙	Nichiren	日蓮
Lun-yü	論語	*Nihon jugakushi*	日本儒学史
Lun-yü chi-chu	論語集註	*Nihon kogakuha*	日本古学派の
Maruyama Masao	丸山眞男	*no tetsugaku*	哲学
Matsudaira	松平藤八郎	*Nihon koten*	日本古典文学
Tōhachirō		*bungaku taikei*	大系
Matsunaga Sekigo	松永尺五	*Nihon meike shisho*	日本名家四書
Meng-tzu	孟子	*chūshaku zensho*	註釈全書
Meng-tzu chi-chu	孟子集註	*Nihon no meicho*	日本の名著
Minamoto Ryōen	源了円	*Nihon rinri ihen*	日本倫理彙篇
Minamoto	源実朝	*Nihon seiji shisōshi*	日本政治思想
Sanetomo		*kenkyū*	史研究
Minamoto Yoriie	源頼家	*Nihon shushigaku*	日本朱子学と
Minamoto	源頼朝	*to chōsen*	朝鮮
Yoritomo		Nihonbashi	日本橋
Minamoto	源義経	*nihonteki shii*	日本的思惟
Yoshitsune		Nishikawa Joken	西川如見
Ming	明	*nō*	能
ming te	明德	Noda Tahei	野田太兵衛
Mito	水戸	Noda Yahei	野田弥兵衛
Miura Chikkei	三浦竹溪	Ogyū Hōan	荻生方庵
Miyake Masahiko	三宅正彦	Ogyū Keiichi	荻生敬一
Mizuno Genrō	水野元朗	Ogyū Sorai	荻生徂徠
Mo-tzu	墨子	*Ogyū Sorai*	荻生年譜考
monozuki	ものずき	*nempukō*	
morosugi	もろすぎ	*Ogyū Sorai zenshū*	荻生徂徠全集
mumyō	無明	Ōishi Shinsaburō	大石慎三郎
Muro Kyūsō	室鳩巣	*okonai*	行ない
Naitō Shūri	内藤修理	Ōmi	近江

oshieru	教える	*Shih-ching shih-pen ku-yi*	詩経世本古義
Pan Ku	班固		
pen-jan chih hsing / honzen no sei	本然之性	*Shih-ching shuo-yüeh*	詩経説約
Pien Ch'üeh	扁鵲	*shih-kao / sekkō*	石膏
rikutsu	理屈	Shimada Kenji	島田虔次
Rongochō	論語徴	Shimamura Kenshuku	島村謙叔
Saitō Shōichi	斎藤正一		
Sakai Tadayori	酒井忠寄	*shinnyo*	眞如
Sakai Tadazane	酒井忠眞	Shinran	親鸞
Sakata	酒田	*shintai*	眞諦
samurai dokoro	侍所	*shite*	仕手
San-t'i shih-chi	三体詩集	*shōgi*	将棋
Satō Naokata	佐藤直方	*Shōnai-han*	庄内藩
Seidan	政談	*Shu-ching*	書経
Shang	商	*Shu-ching chi-ch'uan*	書経集伝
Shang-shu t'ung-kao	尚書通考	*shu-fa / shohō*	書法
Shao	韶	*Shu-ts'ai shih-ch'uan p'ang-t'ung*	書蔡氏伝旁通
Shen Nung	神農		
Shen Pu-hai	申不害		
shi	子	Shun	舜
Shiba	芝	*Sorai sensei tōmonsho*	徂徠先生答問書
shih / koto	事		
Shih-chi	史記	*Soraigaku—jugaku kara bungaku e*	徂徠学―儒学から文学へ
Shih chi-ch'uan	詩集伝		
Shih-chih t'ung-chien	資治通鑑	*Soraigaku no kisoteki kenkyū*	徂徠学の基礎的研究
Shih-chih t'ung-chien kang-mu	資治通鑑綱目	Ssu-ma Ch'ien	司馬遷
		Ssu-ma Kuang	司馬光
Shih-ching chi-ch'uan	詩経集伝	Ssu-ma Ni	司馬牛
		Ssu-ma T'an	司馬談
Shih-ching chu-ch'uan	詩経朱伝	Su Tung-p'o	蘇東坡
		Sugiyama	杉山

sugoroku	双六	*Tokugawa shisō*	徳川思想小史
Sun Fu	孫復	*shōshi*	
Sun-tzu	孫子	*Tokugawa shisō-*	徳川思想史
Sung	宋	*shi kenkyū*	研究
Ta-hsüeh	大学	Tokugawa	徳川綱吉
Ta-hsüeh chang-	大学章句	Tsunayoshi	
chü		Tokugawa	徳川吉宗
Ta-hsüeh huo-wen	大学或問	Yoshimune	
ta-wu / ōsatori	大悟	*torika*	取簡
Tahara Tsuguo	田原嗣郎	Ts'ai Ch'en	蔡沈
T'ai Kung-wang	太公望	Ts'ai Shu	蔡叔
T'ai-tsung	太宗	*Tso-ch'uan*	左伝
Taiheisaku	太平策	*tso-wei / sakui*	作為
Taihō	大法	Tsuji Tatsuya	辻達也
Taira	平	Tsuruoka	鶴岡
Takeda Shingen	武田信玄	*T'ung Tien*	通典
T'ang	唐	*tzu-jan / shizen*	自然
T'ang Shih-hsüan	唐詩選	*tz'u-pei / jihi*	慈悲
T'ang-shih p'in-hui	唐詩品彙	Tzu Ssu	子思
tao / michi	道	Tzu Yu	子游
Tatebayashi	館林	Uesugi Kenshin	上杉謙信
te / toku	徳	*unka mushi*	雲霞虫
Tendai	天台	*utsuru*	移る
Ti-fan	帝範	Wada Yoshimori	和田義盛
Ti K'u	帝嚳	*waka*	和歌
t'ien-li / tenri	天理	*waki*	脇
t'ien-ti tzu-jan /	天地自然	Wang An-shih	王安石
tenchi shizen		Wang I	王逸
t'ien-ti tzu-jan chih	天地自然之道	Wang Mang	王莽
tao / tenchi shizen		Wang Yang-ming	王陽明
no michi		Wang Yüan-mei,	王元美, 世貞
to	斗	Shih-chen	
Tōkaidō	東海道	*waza*	わざ
Tokugawa gōri	徳川合理思想	Wen	文
shisō no keifu	の系譜	*Wen-hsüan*	文選

Wu	武	Yang Tsung-yüan	柳子元
wu/mono	物	Yao	堯
Wu-ch'eng	武城	*yashinau*	養う
Wu Tsa Tsu	五雜俎	Yasui Shōtarō	安井小太郎
Wu-tzu	吳子	Yen Yüan	顏元
Yabu Shin-an	藪震菴	*Yi Chou-shu*	逸周書
Yakubun sentei	訳文筌蹄	*Yi-li*	儀礼
Yamaga Sokō	山鹿素行	Yi T'oegye	李退溪
Yamagata	山形	*Ying-k'ui lü-sui*	瀛奎律髓
Yamagata ken-shi	山形県史	Yōrō	養老
Yamagata Masakage	山県昌景	Yoshikawa Kōjirō	吉川幸次郎
Yamaji Aizan	山路愛山	Yu	禹
Yamazaki Ansai	山崎闇斎	*Yüan*	元
Yanagisawa Yasu-aki (Yoshiyasu)	柳沢保明 (吉保)	Yuasa Jōzan	湯浅常山
Yang Chu	楊朱	*yung-jen*	庸人
		yung/yū	勇

INDEX

References to the translation are in **boldface**.

About the Author

Samuel Hideo Yamashita received his Ph.D. from the University of Michigan in 1981 and is associate professor of history at Pomona College. He was a postdoctoral fellow at the Edwin O. Reischauer Institute of Japanese Studies at Harvard University and a senior tutor in East Asian Studies there before taking a position at Pomona. Professor Yamashita has written several articles on the ancient learning movement. His research interests include Confucian academies in the early modern period, warrior vendettas, and the modern Japanese state's appropriation of Confucian and warrior discourses.

Production Notes

Composition and paging were done in
FrameMaker software on an AGFA AccuSet
Postscript Imagesetter by the design
and production staff of University of
Hawaii Press.

The text typeface is Sabon
and the display
typeface is Gill Sans.

Offset presswork and binding were done by
The Maple-Vail Book Manufacturing Group.
Text paper is Glatfelter Offset Vellum, basis 50.